MEN-AT-ARMS SERIES

EDITOR: MARTIN WINDROW

# The British Army 1914-18

## Text by
### R. J. MARRION and
### D. S. V. FOSTEN

## Colour plates by
### G. A. EMBLETON

D1066212

OSPREY PUBLISHING LONDON

Published in 1978 by
Osprey Publishing Ltd
Member company of the George Philip Group
12–14 Long Acre, London WC2E 9LP
© Copyright 1978 Osprey Publishing Ltd
Reprinted 1981, 1982, 1983, 1984, 1985, 1986
1987

ISBN 0 85045 287 2

Filmset by BAS Printers Limited,
Over Wallop, Hampshire
Printed in Hong Kong

## Introduction

Between 1869 and 1874, Edward Cardwell, Gladstone's Secretary for War, undertook several major reforms to modernise and re-organise the British Army. The Crimean War, and the campaigns quelling the Mutiny in India, had revealed serious administrative and command shortcomings; Cardwell's legislation was aimed at curing these faults and was to serve as the foundation of a new-style army which, by 1914, developed into the best professional fighting force in Europe.

One important innovation was abolition of the commission purchase system. Another was the amendment of the period of service for NCOs and men, now reduced from twenty-one years to seven with the Colours and three on the reserve (three with the Colours and nine on the reserve for the Foot Guards). Under Cardwell, control of the artillery and Royal Engineers passed to the Commander-in-Chief. The Transport and Commissariat also passed from civilian contracting to army control, and the Army Service Corps and Ordnance Stores Department evolved.

Fundamental to the new infantry structure was the bracketing of most regiments of the line into new regiments, each of two battalions (the twenty-five senior regiments already had two battalions). The new regiments, made up of 'paired' battalions, one from each of two old regiments, lost their pre-1881 numbered titles which linked their seniority with ancient lineage and past successes on the field. Instead they received new County or City titles, linking regiments geographically to areas from which they were expected to recruit. Initially this proved a most unpopular reform. The old num-

**Grenadier Guards officers en route for the front, 1914; note rank badges on shoulder straps, rather than on cuffs as worn by line officers. (Courtesy Officer Commanding Grenadier Guards)**

The standard '02 khaki field service dress for infantry (right) and cavalry. The private of the Herefordshire Regt. (Territorials) wears the leather waistbelt of the 1914 equipment; the trooper of the 10th Hussars wears pantaloons with puttees tied at the ankle, spurs, and the '03 bandolier. (R. Harris; R. Marrion)

bered regiments became the 1st or 2nd battalions of the new units, and arguments were fierce as each struggled to maintain its old seniority under modern titles. Henceforth all infantry regiments had two battalions, except for the Foot Guards (who had three each), the Rifle Brigade and King's Royal Rifle Corps (who had four each).

A system was also evolved by which one battalion of a regiment served overseas, while the other remained on Home Station. Complicated systems were worked out to ensure fair distribution of duties. The home service battalions provided reinforcements for battalions overseas and consequently were often under strength.

Besides losing their numbers, regiments also lost their ancient facings, and this caused added resentment. Henceforth, all English regiments had white; Scottish, yellow; Irish, green; and Royal Regiments, blue facings. Many regiments never could accept this ruling and protests became so strong, especially from regiments such as the Buffs and Green Howards, that many were eventually permitted to resume their traditional facings.

There were, however, still no fundamental reforms in tactics or training methods. Lessons were not learned from the many small colonial wars. Consequently, when the major Boer War developed, the army was still drilled and deployed much in the manner of the early 19th century. The Boer War was a severe test for Cardwell's reforms. Most proved well justified; but besides tactics, other defects were revealed, especially in the structure of the senior command. Cardwell's successors, up to Haldane (1905–12), did much to remedy these by such measures as creating the Imperial General Staff, abolishing the post of Commander-in-Chief, and developing the reserve structure.

Tactics eventually developed against the Boers, especially those fostered by Lord Roberts, led to infantry training which placed more emphasis on an ability to shoot straight and fast, and on mobility. The mounted infantry arm was significantly expanded; men were drilled in new methods of attack, defence, and withdrawal, and were taught to take more advantage of cover. The introduction of the Lee-Enfield magazine rifle gave increased opportunities to teach troops to fire rapidly, accurately and with such devastating effect that enemy troops at Mons thought they were facing machine-guns.

As part of restructuring the reserve, the old Volunteer Force was dissolved and a 'Territorial' Army created. The Militia became a Special Reserve, with one or more battalions formed on each regular line regiment. Cavalry Volunteers (Yeomanry) became part of the new Territorial Army. Initially, fourteen Divisions of Territorial Infantry and fifteen Brigades of Yeomanry Cavalry were formed. A formidable force of Territorial Artillery was gradually created, consisting of fifty-four brigades of Field; twelve batteries of Horse; and sixteen batteries of Heavy Artillery, the whole force led by cadres of regular officers and permanent staffs of senior NCO instructors from regular formations. The Territorial Army was administered by County Associations. In addition to the regulars the army now had a further reserve of retired Regular officers; a Special Reserve structured from the old Militia; the volunteer Territorial Army and, from 1910, the so-called National Reserve—a voluntary register of men of all ranks who could be available for duty in emergency.

The well-tried Prussian system of dividing the country into military areas was established. Known as 'Commands', these had Regular, Special Reserve, and Territorial units allotted to each. The infantry was formed in six divisions, the cavalry into one, each formation with its own divisional artillery, engineer, communications, and medical support. An anomaly was that the efficient Territorial force had no statutory liability to serve

Maxim gun crew, 1914; at this time every infantry unit had a section of two guns served by an officer and twelve men, mostly expert marksmen. For each gun 3,500 rounds were carried, with another 8,000 in reserve. The Maxim and carriage weighed approx. 9½cwt, and fired 500rpm. Late in 1915 it was gradually replaced by the Vickers, weighing 40lbs and firing 500rpm. After the formation of the Machine Gun Corps during the war infantry and cavalry units received increased firepower with the issue of the Lewis LMG, weighing 28½lbs and fed from 47-round drums. This was air-cooled, with an outer casing of aluminium and a radiator.

overseas unless units volunteered to the Lords-Lieutenant of their Counties under a 'General Service' obligation. (However, on the outbreak of hostilities 90% of the force volunteered en masse.)

In 1914 the Regular Establishment numbered some 125,000 officers and men and comprised four regiments of Foot Guards; sixty-nine line infantry regiments; three Household and twenty-five line cavalry regiments. The artillery comprised 147 Field; twenty-five Horse; ninety-eight Heavy (Fortress and Siege), and nine Mountain Batteries. There were forty-three Army Service Corps Horse Transport Companies, twenty-one Mechanical Transport Companies, five Supply Companies and four Remount units. There were thirty-eight companies of the Royal Army Medical Corps and Veterinary Staff, attached to most units together with companies of the Army Ordnance Corps, Army Pay Corps, Corps of Military Police and a Staff Provost Corps. The Royal Engineers, besides its ten Depots and fifty-nine Companies covering every possible service, possessed an Air Battalion which later became the Royal Flying Corps, with a military wing of seven squadrons, five of which went to France with the BEF.

Shortly before the outbreak of the war a double-company system was introduced and thereafter each battalion comprised four companies, the senior NCO of each being a Company Sergeant

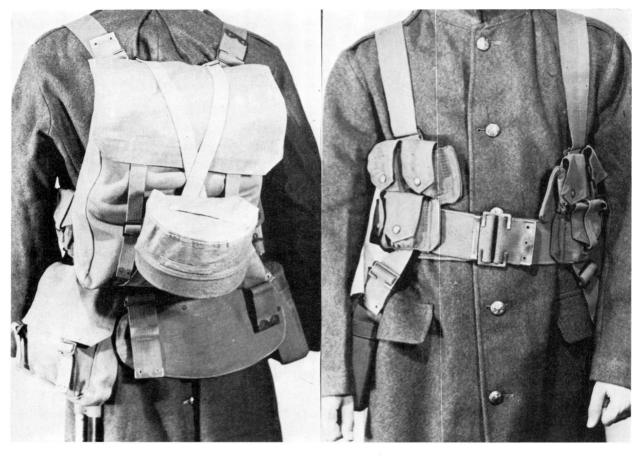

Major. Intensive training at troop, gun and platoon level took place during winter. When the weather broke in spring men were exercised by battery, squadron and company; in summer they moved on to brigade and battalion training, and the season ended in full scale divisional and brigade manoeuvres in the autumn.

In 1914 infantry training was based on the maxim that the cardinal virtues were firepower and movement, but troops were still taught to fire from extended lines; sections advanced at the double while covering fire was given by the remainder of the company. Behind each firing line were support lines and finally reserves. All advanced by stages until the objective was reached; volleys were fired, followed by a rousing bayonet charge. The manuals were of course full of variations on this theme. Entrenching tools were issued and men instructed in their use although few, if any, could have foretold how important these tools were to be in just a few years' time.

During the small wars the cavalry had learnt the

**Pattern 1908 Web Infantry Equipment—a major advance in design, which placed no restriction on the chest, and which could be removed in one piece if desired. Ten sets were successfully tested in India in 1907. It consisted of a 3in-wide waistbelt, two 2in-wide braces with buckles, a pair of cartridge carriers each with five pouches, bayonet frog, waterbottle carrier, haversack, pack, pack supporting straps, and entrenching tool carriers for head and shaft. The canvas-covered canteen is seen slung on the rear face of the pack. By October 1914 it was found that rounds were being lost from the bottom left-hand pouch; soldiers leaning on trench parapets to fire were snagging the press-stud. An immediate modification provided a sliding strap for the bottom carriers, with the press-stud on top of the flap. (IWM Collection, photo R. Marrion)**

value of dismounted fire action. The British reply to the Boer commando was the mounted infantry, and subsequent cavalry training was aimed at emulating their tactics. Cavalry action during the War varied according to the theatre of operations. In France the cavalry could be used only as infantry during stagnant trench-warfare periods. However, in the early months, and more especially in the latter stages, in the great advances in 1918, they returned more to their traditional function, and became once more the 'eyes and ears' of the infantry.

In August and September 1914, six divisions of

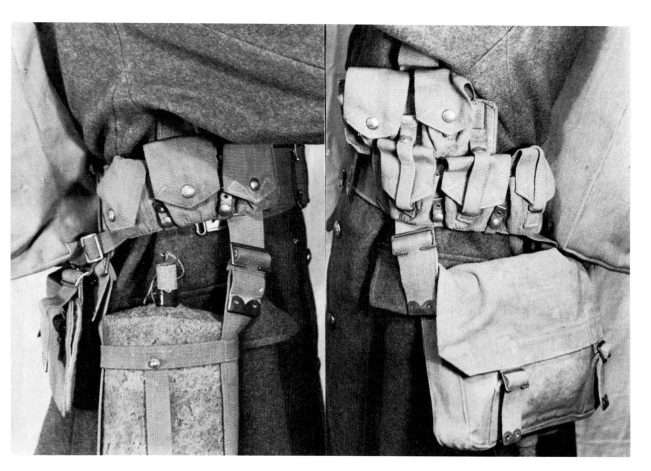

infantry, plus the Cavalry Division, formed the British Expeditionary Force (BEF). On arrival in France the force was grouped into three Army Corps. Mobilisation continued; battalions stationed abroad were brought home, recruitment expanded, and, by spring of 1915, there were eleven divisions of regular infantry in the field.

However, it soon became clear that even this expanded force needed more support, and Territorial divisions were in France by early 1915, others being despatched to the Middle East. One of Kitchener's first duties as Secretary for War was to call for a further '100,000 volunteers'. A brilliant administrator, he had, mistakenly, small regard for the Territorial Army, considering it fit only for home service duties. With such small appreciation of the toughness, morale and ésprit de corps of the 'Terriers', he concentrated on recruiting his new volunteers into 'Service' battalions, to be added to the strength of the regulars in the field.

Called 'New Army' formations, and including many so-called 'Pals' Battalions, these were in-

itially led by officers of the Indian Army on leave in Britain, with junior commissioned officers from Officer Training Corps of schools, universities, or public schools. Enthusiasm ran high; cities, towns, industry, universities and local authorities all flocked to raise units and provide finance to support them. By the end of 1914, 1,190,000 volunteers had come forward. Existing regular army administration could not cope with this enormous influx; hastily mustered formations were poorly trained, drilled by often-meagre cadres of elderly officers and NCOs, and commanded by officers mostly called from retirement for the purpose. They spent frustrating months in makeshift camps, dressed in civilian clothes or cheap blue smocks. Enthusiasm waned, and finally recruitment all but dried up. Meantime, the decimated BEF continued fighting magnificently against great odds, supported ably by the Territorials with added support from newly arrived Dominion formations; but France still carried a very heavy burden.

It was clear that Kitchener's solution was

unsatisfactory, and Lord Derby was appointed Director General of Recruitment. He introduced conscription and his ensuing 'Derby Scheme' was initially for unmarried men, attested according to age. However, even this scheme proved unsuccessful in sustaining replacements for enormous casualty lists, and the subsequent Act of 1916 resulted in all single men between eighteen and forty-one years of age becoming liable for service. In May the same year continuing losses made it necessary to pass more stringent legislation until finally, in April 1918, the ultimate Act made it statutory to call men for service up to fifty-one years of age. By this means the army was expanded until, by autumn 1918, some regiments had nearly fifty battalions in the field. There were seventy divisions of infantry,

and the artillery had increased in even greater proportion, with nearly 50,000 all ranks and over 6,000 guns. Cavalry also expanded, though not in the same proportion, and support troops—especially the Service Corps, Signals and Ordnance Corps—grew enormously. By the end of the war the infantry alone had a paper strength of nearly 2,000,000 officers and men.

The machine-gun had especially proved its importance, resulting in the establishment of a separate Corps to deploy its potential. In 1916 it was considered important enough to warrant its own Inspectorate. In 1914, the infantry had one machine-gun to every 500 men in the field; by 1918, there was one gun deployed for every twenty men. Tanks, a formidable British invention, thought by many to have been the decisive factor in the final Allied victory, appeared in action for the first time on the Somme in 1916. (The name 'tank' was initially given because the rhomboidal metal shapes seemed like water cisterns or supply tanks; the name stuck for security reasons.) The Mark I

**Early in the war, before enough sets of webbing were available, a substitute set was issued—initially to troops in training, but in the event, to many combat units of 'Kitchener's Army'. It was entirely of brown leather, and followed the design of the webbing except for the pouches, which resembled the old Slade-Wallace set. The haversack and pack were of webbing fitted with leather straps. Here the '1914 Leather Equipment' is seen worn with the greatcoat. (IWM Collection, photo R. Marrion)**

had 10cm armour plate, a crew of eight, weighed 28 tons, and was armed with two 6-pdr Hotchkiss guns. This was the 'male tank'; a lighter-armed version armed with three Hotchkiss machine guns was termed the 'female'. It had a speed of about 3mph. Other Marks followed, including the IV, and V; the VI and VII were designs which never saw action. There were also 'medium' tanks and armoured cars, and a final Anglo-American tank called the Mk. VIII which was never used by either army during the war.

# Command Structure

The Chief of the Imperial General Staff and Commanders-in-Chief in the field were Field Marshals. Army commanders were generals; corps commanders, lieutenant-generals; and divisional commanders, major-generals. The power and responsibility of co-ordinating staff was vested in the Commander-in-Chief at General Headquarters. He in turn delegated authority as he thought fit to his Chief of General Staff. The Staff was organised as three branches:

## The General Staff Branch (GS)
Responsible for all military operations, embarkation, landings, organisation and efficiency. Selection of sites for operations. Communication in the field. Acquisition of information about the enemy. Advice on movements. Supply and parking of guns and vehicles, etc.

## The Adjutant General's Branch (AG)
Responsible for discipline, military law, appointment and promotion of officers, internal economy, pay, promotions, honours, enlistment, spiritual welfare, provision of medical supplies, sanitation, casualties, ceremonials, routine garrisons, camp duties, etc.

## Quarter Master General's Branch (QMG)
Responsible for all supplies, ammunition, equipment, clothing, stores of all kinds except medical equipment, land, railway and sea transportation, remounts, veterinary and postal services, accounting for expenditure, etc.

# Composition

Early in 1916 there were four Armies in France. Each had an establishment of four Corps comprising three Divisions each. The principal difference between an Army or Corps on the one hand, and a Division on the other, was that the former were merely headquarters units forming part of the chain of command only. They did not hold units on a permanent basis. Divisions usually retained the same brigades, and brigades their battalions, on an all but permanent basis.

Consequently, the ordinary soldier seldom knew which Army or which Corps his battalion/brigade/division belonged to at any given time. He was a 'Dorset', a 'Buff' or a 'Gloster', and his battalion became his 'home'. He often remained with it, in the same sector of the line, for months at a time. Tours of duty would be from four to eight days in the trenches, longer at times of stress. When not in action, the battalion would be taken back through support trenches to billets to rest. In the event this often meant endless labouring, fatigue duties or carrying parties. Most hated duties were wiring parties, and hazardous patrols at night. During quiet periods battalions could expect to lose about thirty men a month from death, wounds and sickness. The following are the establishments prior to the outbreak of the war.

## INFANTRY

### The Infantry Division
Commanded by a lieutenant-general or major-general. Normally comprised three brigades, each of four battalions; three Field, one Field Howitzer and one Heavy Artillery Brigade. An Ammunition Column, a Divisional Ammunition Column; two Field Companies and one Signal Company RE; a Divisional Train; three Field Ambulances and a Pioneer Battalion (to provide labour for the Field Companies although also used as fighting units). Total strength on mobilization, 598 officers and 18,077 NCOs and men.

### The Infantry Brigade
Commanded by a brigadier-general with an HQ comprising 4 officers and 20 NCOs and men. The

four battalions had a total strength of 120 officers and 3,968 NCOs and men.

### The Infantry Battalion

Commanded by a lieutenant-colonel. It had a strength on concentration of 1,000 officers and men and a fighting strength of about 800. The battalion comprised an HQ company and four rifle companies each commanded by majors (often captains because of casualty rate). Support sections were Signals, Pioneers, Bearers and Provost.

### The Infantry Company

Commanded by captains, lieutenants or second-lieutenants due to casualty rates. Had a strength of 240 NCOs and men, divided into four platoons each of 60 men.

### The Infantry Platoon

Commanded by an NCO, either a sergeant or corporal, and divided into four sections each of 14 men.

There were also Machine-Gun Companies and Light Trench Mortar Batteries in support. Personnel of both were infantrymen armed with standard weapons. At the outbreak of war every battalion had its own MG section comprising two Maxim guns served by an officer and twelve other ranks. The guns were mule-carried and the section was divided into two teams. Gunners had to be expert riflemen. Late in 1915 the Maxim was replaced by the Vickers, and these were concentrated under divisional control.

*Divisional Train*: 26 officers, 630 other ranks. *Horses*: 66 riding, 597 draught. *Carts*: 17. *Waggons*: 127. *Motor cars*: 4. *Bicycles*: 30.

## CAVALRY

### The Cavalry Division

Completely autonomous and comprising four Cavalry Brigades; two Horse Artillery Brigades; four Field Troops of Engineers (including Bridging Units); one Signal Squadron; one Train and four Field Ambulances. The Divisional Artillery HQ comprised 3 officers and 15 other ranks, and the two Horse Artillery Brigades, 38 officers with 1,302 other ranks. The Divisional Engineers HQ had a strength of 4 officers and 10 other ranks, and the four Field Troops, 12 officers and 296 other ranks. The

Signals Squadron consisted of 10 officers and 197 men, while the Train had 31 officers and 711 other ranks. The four Field Ambulances had 24 officers and 9,412 other ranks for which 7,362 riding horses, 2,726 draught horses and 107 pack animals were needed.

### The Cavalry Brigade

This had a headquarters comprising 30 officers and 77 other ranks, and a strength of 332 officers and 6,356 other ranks. Each Cavalry Brigade had 24 machine guns attached and the two Horse Artillery Brigades were equipped with 13-pdr quick-firing guns. There were three Cavalry Regiments to a

With both sides consolidating ground held, the winter of 1914/15 saw the onset of trench warfare under conditions which emphasised the deficiencies of clothing and equipment. Protective coats and jerkins of leather and goatskin were issued from early in 1915, as well as waders and other rubber footwear. (Left, courtesy J. Woodroff; centre, IWM)

Brigade, each Regiment comprising three Squadrons each of 6 officers and 149 rank and file, plus HQ staff and Machine Gun section; a total regimental strength of 26 officers and 514 other ranks.

Besides the Cavalry Brigade proper, there were mixed brigades, known as Mounted Brigades which included (a) two Cavalry Regiments and one Mounted Infantry Battalion or (b) one Cavalry Regiment and two Mounted Infantry Battalions.
(a) This type of brigade included an HQ, two Cavalry Regiments, one Horse Artillery Battery, one Brigade Mounted Ammunition Column, one Signal Troop, one Mounted Infantry Battalion, one Brigade Train, one Cavalry Field Ambulance; a combined strength of 108 officers and 2,203 men.
(b) This type of Brigade included an HQ, one Cavalry Regiment, one Horse Artillery Battery, one Mounted Brigade Ammunition Column and one Cavalry Field Ambulance with the same strength as the above.

**The Cavalry Train**
Consisted of 31 officers and 711 other ranks with an establishment of 79 riding horses, 664 draught horses, 27 two-horsed carts, 27 four-horsed waggons, 8 eight-horsed waggons, 5 motor cars and 37 bicycles.

## ARTILLERY

Deployed immediately in the rear of the infantry was the divisional artillery (Royal Field Artillery) comprising eight batteries each of six guns, 75% of which were 18-pdr (13-pdrs in some Territorial units) field guns, the remainder composed of heavy mortars and 4.5in howitzers. The RFA liaised closely with front-line infantry, providing observation officers and signallers in forward observation posts.

Field guns were provided with both high-explosive and shrapnel shells. Shrapnel with timed fuses was used up to a range of about 6,000 yards. Fitted with percussion fuses, shrapnel was used with great effect against troops using walls or parapets of trenches for protection. High-explosive was used chiefly against more elaborate defences including dugouts and redoubts or protected gun emplacements. Field-howitzers also fired both shrapnel and HE, using shrapnel charges up to about 6,000 yards with an air explosive range of about 7,000 yards.

The heavy and medium artillery were under Army or Corps control. Corps artillery also controlled four batteries of medium mortars. Heavy guns fired both types of shell mentioned above, but of greater weight and up to ranges of 9,000 yards, the extreme range of their guns being about 10,000 yards.

The components and strength of Royal Artillery units was as follows:

**Horse Artillery** (attached to cavalry divisions):
BRIGADE: 19 officers, 651 other ranks. *Horses*: 275 riding, 480 draught. *Guns*: 12 × 13-pdrs. *Carts*: 4. *Waggons*: 64. *Bicycles*: 12.

BATTERY: 5 officers, 199 other ranks. *Horses*: 102 riding, 122 draught. *Guns*: 6. *Carts*: 1. *Waggons*: 38. *Bicycles*: 3.

**Horse Artillery Ammunition Column**: 4 officers, 219 other ranks. *Horses*: 44 riding, 228 draught. *Carts*: 1. *Waggons*: 38. *Bicycles*: 3.

**Field Artillery**:
18-pdr BRIGADE: 23 officers, 766 other ranks. *Horses*: 195 riding, 537 draught. *Guns*: 18. *Carts*: 12. *Waggons*: 60. *Bicycles*: 5.

18-pdr BATTERY: 5 officers, 194 other ranks. *Horses*: 20 riding, 163 draught. *Guns*: 6. *Carts*: 1. *Waggons*: 12. *Bicycles*: 1.

4.5in HOWITZER BRIGADE: 22 officers, 734 other ranks. *Horses*: 190 riding, 502 draught. *Guns*: 18. *Carts*: 5. *Waggons*: 57. *Bicycles*: 5.

4.5in HOWITZER BATTERY: 5 officers, 194 other ranks. *Horses*: 50 riding, 122 draught. *Guns*: 6. *Carts*: 1. *Waggons*: 12. *Bicycles*: 1.

**Heavy Artillery**:
BATTERY: 5 officers, 153 other ranks. *Horses*: 22 riding, 97 draught. *Guns*: 4. *Carts*: 1. *Waggons*: 12. *Bicycles*: 1.

**Siege Artillery**:
6in HOWITZER BRIGADE: 30 officers, 949 other ranks. *Horses*: 102 riding, 497 draught. *Guns*: 16. *Carts*: 16. *Waggons*: 72.

\* \* \*

### The Royal Engineers

The Royal Engineers had two responsibilities at divisional level. Their signal companies were responsible for communications between units and divisions, although both infantry and artillery provided their own internal signal support. Field companies of Royal Engineers were responsible for the supervision of construction and maintenance of trenches, dug-outs and the storage of ammunition within the trench system, although most of the manual labour was carried out by infantry, at night, in the role of carrying and wiring parties in the forward areas.

A Field Company of Engineers comprised 6 officers and 211 other ranks; a Field Troop, 3 officers and 74 other ranks; a Field Company Section, 1 officer and 43 men. Transport for a Field Company consisted of 17 riding horses, 55 draught horses, 4 pack horses, 14 two-horsed carts, 1 four-horsed waggon, 3 six-horsed waggons and 33 cycles.

### The Signals Service

*Signals Squadron*: 10 officers and 197 other ranks; 80 riding horses, 68 draught horses; 14 pack horses; 1 two-horsed cart; 9 two-horsed waggons; 3 four-horsed waggons; 5 six-horsed waggons; 2 motor cars; 6 motorcycles; 34 bicycles.

Signals squadrons were divided into four troops titled 'A', 'B', 'C' and 'D'; there were also troops

*above* Three examples of Highland officers' dress. All wear the cutaway khaki doublet with gauntlet cuff; the officer on the right seems to wear the original version of the officers' tunic with fastened collar. The officer on the left wears tartan trews, and the centre figure the kilt, apron, hose, and khaki spats. The right hand figure wears tartan pantaloons, leather gaiters and spurred boots for mounted duties.

*right* Officers' (top) and other ranks' versions of the Highland pattern of '02 khaki service dress, worn here by a subaltern and private of the Seaforth Highlanders. (R. Marrion)

*below* Group of Highlanders in August 1915. All wear full marching order and the standard '02 service jacket—only the man second from left appears to have the Scots cutaway skirts. The sergeant, left, wears the khaki tam-o'-shanter, while the others appear to wear the smaller Balmoral bonnet.

with specific duties with cavalry brigades, mounted brigades, and responsibility for wireless, air lines, cable carrying, etc. 'A' Troop was responsible for intercommunication between cavalry divisional HQ and GHQ, and comprised two wireless waggon stations. 'B' Troop was responsible for general intercommunication with the cavalry division and was to keep in touch with divisional HQ and the wireless stations serving it or the permanent telegraph system. It consisted of two cable detachments with twenty-eight miles of cable and eight vibrator offices. 'C' Troop was responsible for intercommunication between divisional HQ and brigades or contact squadrons. It comprised one wireless (waggon) station and two wireless (pack) stations. 'D' Troop was responsible for visual signalling and despatch riding services in conjunction with the means of intercommunication. It comprised twelve mounted men, twenty-eight bicyclists, six motorcyclists and two motor cars.

## The Royal Army Medical Corps

The Royal Army Medical Corps was responsible for all medical services from the front line to areas beyond the range of the enemy guns. The most forward units were the Battalion Medical Officers supported by a few orderlies; they occupied dugouts within the front-line trench system and dispensed first-aid only. All but the lightest cases were evacuated to Field Ambulances, usually behind the front line, where wounds could be dressed. There were no facilities for any form of surgery, the main function being to get wounded back to Casualty Clearing Stations beyond the range of enemy guns and outside the battle area. Divisional Field Ambulances comprised 10 officers and 242 other ranks, 14 riding horses and 86 draught horses, 7 carts and 16 four-horsed ambulances.

The Director of Medical Services was responsible for all medical and sanitary services for the army in the field, and each division had an Assistant Director and a Deputy Assistant.

## Supply

The Director of Supply was responsible for the provision of food, forage, etc., for the army in the field. The object was to effect supply by rail or mechanical transport, delivering daily to Army Service Corps units and thence to the troops. Main supply depots were established at advance bases or convenient positions on the railways; they were maintained by rail from home bases or from supplies collated from the nearby countryside. Field Bakeries and Butcheries were established at advanced bases or at points on the railway other than main regulating stations.

On arrival at rendezvous, supply columns were ordered by representatives of HQ concerned to proceed to refilling points situated in localities which, if convenient, could either be near the front of the areas from which the division, etc., moved, or at suitable localities well in advance of these areas. When troops were stationary, except in battle situations, it was normally considered preferable to send supply columns into brigade areas where refilling points were placed. During battle it was usually necessary to send back the Train some distance where they refilled from supply columns. Horsed Reserve Parks, each capable of carrying two days reserve of iron ration and two days grain for a division, were maintained in the rear areas for emergencies.

At the beginning of the war the ASC consisted of 500 officers and 6,000 men; by the Armistice it had increased to 4,408 officers and 311,478 other ranks.

## Ammunition Supply

Responsibility for supply of ammunition in the field was divided between Ordnance Corps units working under direct command of General Headquarters and similar but smaller units with divisions, cavalry divisions or other formations. Reserves of ammunition held by fighting troops were divided into three lines:

Regimental Reserve, carried on pack animals (each infantry company had a brace of mules to carry small arms ammunition) or first-line transport vehicles. Ammunition expended in the firing line was replaced from this source.

Divisional Ammunition Columns, forming part of each Artillery Brigade. With the exception of the Howitzer Brigade and Heavy Battery Ammunition Columns, they carried both small arms and artillery ammunition. Regimental reserves were replaced from this source.

*Divisional Ammunition Columns*, forming part of the Divisional Artillery, Brigade or Heavy Battery Ammunition Columns were replaced from these columns, except in the case of the Cavalry Division and Army Troops who received their ammunition direct from the park.

Divisional Ammunition Columns were divided into a Headquarters and four sections. The first three contained 18-pdr and small arms ammunition, the fourth section, 4.5in howitzer and 60-pdr ammunition.

An infantry brigade normally formed its ammunition reserve by detaching from each battalion about a third of its regimental reserve under a selected officer. This formed a link between the regimental reserve and the Artillery Brigade Ammunition Column. On the lines of communication, ammunition reserves were divided between the Parks and Ordnance Depots.

The fundamental principle involved was that troops in action should never have to go back for ammunition. It was the business of rear formations to send it forward. During an action ammunition parks were sent forward under orders of General Headquarters, to a rendezvous. From these points, sections or even small elements of the parks were sent further forward to arrange refilling points, fixed by the divisional staff, where the replenishment of the divisional supply column was carried out.

The position of brigade ammunition columns during actions was normally regulated by artillery

The sudden influx of volunteers answering Kitchener's appeal strained the supplies of khaki uniforms, and 'blue smock' uniforms were issued temporarily to recruits. This photograph shows the blue smock outfit worn with blue sidecaps by an intake of the 12th Northumberland Fusiliers. The uniform was sent for the use of POWs, and after the war was issued to inmates of criminal lunatic asylums. (Courtesy Mrs M. Nethercote)

brigade commanders and was usually about a mile in the rear of the battery waggon lines.

## Army Veterinary Corps

In a war where transportation still relied mainly on horse-drawn vehicles, including transportation of guns for the artillery, and many riding horses were used, including a large cavalry arm, the medical care of the horse was the lot of the Army Veterinary Corps. For its services during the war the Corps was granted the title 'Royal', *vide* Army Order 362 of 1918. Overall control was the responsibility of the Director of Veterinary Services who received instructions from QMG Branch of the Staff. He was assisted by a Deputy Director and represented by an Assistant Director at divisional level.

Veterinary battalions were sub-divided into four companies, each comprising 6 officers and 221 men, each company known by the letter 'A', 'B', 'C' or 'D'. 'A' Company was commanded by the junior major, the remainder by senior captains with a junior captain as second in command. Each company was divided into four platoons, consecutively numbered 1–16 throughout the bat-

Two examples of the coloured cloth divisional, corps, brigade and regimental insignia which began to proliferate from 1915; the variations, and changes, were far too numerous and inadequately recorded for a comprehensive list to be given, but the commentary on the colour plates includes representative signs. Higher command signs were normally observed on the upper sleeves and sometimes on helmet sides, worn by all ranks; regimental signs (sometimes but not necessarily in a form resembling the unit cap-badge) were sometimes worn on the helmet and usually worn on the back below the collar, particularly by officers, for obvious reasons; eg, the Royal Dublin Fusiliers wore a red triangle as part of 29th Division, or a green shamrock as part of 16th Division, with a blue diamond on the back and on the helmet sides.

talion, and commanded by a subaltern. In turn, the platoon was sub-divided into sections, again numbered 1–16 through the company and commanded by a sergeant or corporal. Senior NCOs, Company Sergeant Majors and Company Quartermaster Sergeants were respectively immediate assistants to the Company Commanders and seconds in command. The four senior sergeants were the Platoon Sergeants and acted in a similar capacity to the subalterns.

### Remount Service

The Director of Remounts was responsible for the provision, training, and distribution of all animals used in the field, and for the administration of remount personnel. He was directly responsible to the QMG Branch of the Staff.

### Provost Marshal

Under instruction from the Adjutant General's Branch, the Provost Marshal was responsible for all police duties of the army in the field and for ensuring that military police were distributed to the best advantage. Each detachment of military police was commanded by the Assistant Provost Marshal of the division to which it was attached.

Military police responsibility was to arrest any soldier found without a pass, plundering, making unlawful requisitions, or committing any other offences of any kind. They collected stragglers and guarded against enemy agents; in cases of emergency they could call on any soldier or officer to assist them in supplying guards, sentries or patrols. In 1914, the Provost Marshal in Indian garrisons still had power to give corporal punishment to any person below the rank of NCO who, in his view, had committed a breach of good order and military discipline. Punishment could not exceed thirty lashes.

# Orders of Battle

In this short work it is impossible to provide comprehensive orders of battle for all theatres. The extracts are consequently restricted to provide a broad breakdown of Corps, Divisions and Brigades in major areas of war. Readers who seek complete listing of units involved should refer to official histories of campaigns.

Staff Captain of the Grenadier Guards on the Western Front. He wears the regimental badge on the steel helmet, and gorget patches. Guards officers preserved the traditional regimental button-spacing on the khaki field service jacket. (Courtesy Officer Commanding Grenadier Guards)

## BRITISH EXPEDITIONARY FORCE
### AUGUST 1914

*Commander in Chief*: Field Marshal Sir J. D. P. French
*Chief of General Staff*: Lieutenant-General Sir A. J. Murray
*Adjutant General*: Major-General Sir C. F. N. Macready
*Quartermaster General*: Major-General Sir W. R. Robertson
*Commanding Royal Artillery*: Major-General W. F. L. Lindsay
*Commanding Royal Engineers*: Brigadier-General J. H. Fowke
*The General Headquarters of Administrative Service and Departments* including Directors of Army Signals, Supplies, Ordnance Services, Transport, Railway Transport, Works, Remounts, Veterinary Services, Medical Services, Army Post, and the Paymaster-in-Chief.

## The Cavalry Division

GOC: Major-General E. H. H. Allenby

| *1st Cavalry Brigade* | *2nd Cavalry Brigade* |
|---|---|
| 2nd Dragoon Guards | 4th Dragoon Guards |
| 5th Dragoon Guards | 9th Lancers |
| 11th Hussars | 18th Hussars |
| 1st Signal Troop | 2nd Signal Troop |

| *3rd Cavalry Brigade* | *4th Cavalry Brigade* |
|---|---|
| 4th Hussars | Composite Regt., |
| 5th Lancers | Household Cavalry |
| 16th Lancers | 6th Dragoon Guards |
| 3rd Signal Troop | 3rd Hussars |
| | 4th Signal Troop |

*5th Cavalry Brigade*
Royal Scots Greys
12th Lancers
20th Hussars
5th Signal Troop
plus Artillery and Divisional Troops.

## FIRST CORPS

GOC: Lieutenant-General Sir Douglas Haig

### 1st Division

GOC: Major-General S. H. Lomax

| *1st (Guards) Brigade* | *2nd Infantry Brigade* |
|---|---|
| 1st Coldstream Guards | 2nd Royal Sussex Regt. |
| 1st Scots Guards | 1st Loyal North |
| 1st Black Watch | Lancashire Regt. |
| 2nd Royal Munster | 1st Northamptonshire |
| Fusiliers | Regt. |
| (in September 1914 the | 2nd KRRC |
| 1st Cameron Highlanders | |
| replaced this battalion) | |

*3rd Infantry Brigade*
1st Queen's (Royal West Surrey) Regt.
1st South Wales Borderers
1st Gloucestershire Regt.
2nd Welch Regt.
plus Artillery and Divisional Troops including 'A' Squadron 15th Hussars and the 1st Cyclist Company.

Group of soldiers wearing the ORs' version of the ear-flapped 'trench cap', with the flaps fastened across the crown, and the single-breasted infantryman's greatcoat. Cavalry and mounted units wore a shorter, double-breasted greatcoat. Officers of all arms wore a double-breasted greatcoat, besides many other custom-made trench coats and overcoats. Ranking was worn on the shoulder straps of the official officer's greatcoat, rather than on the cuffs, and the shoulder straps were also piped in arm-of-service colours, eg scarlet (infantry, Rifles, Royal Engineers), yellow (cavalry), blue (Royal Artillery), and white (ASC, RAMC, AVC, CMP, and APC).

### 2nd Division
GOC: Major-General C. C. Monro

*4th (Guards) Brigade*
2nd Grenadier Guards
2nd Coldstream Guards
3rd Coldstream Guards
1st Irish Guards

*5th Infantry Brigade*
2nd Worcestershire Regt.
2nd Oxs and Bucks Light Infantry
2nd Highland Light Infantry
2nd Connaught Rangers

*6th Infantry Brigade*
1st Kings (Liverpool) Regt.
2nd South Staffordshire Regt.
1st Royal Berkshire Regt.
1st KRRC
plus Artillery and Divisional Troops including 'B' Squadron 15th Hussars and the 2nd Cyclist Company.

## SECOND CORPS

GOC: Lieutenant-General Sir J. M. Grierson
(died 17 August 1914)
General Sir H. L. Smith-Dorrien
(from 21 August 1914)

### 3rd Division
GOC: Major-General Hubert I. W. Hamilton

*7th Infantry Brigade*
3rd Worcestershire Regt.
2nd South Lancashire Regt.
1st Duke of Edinburgh's (Wiltshire) Regt.
2nd Royal Irish Rifles

*8th Infantry Brigade*
2nd Royal Scots
2nd Royal Irish Regt.
4th Middlesex Regt.
1st Gordon Highlander (replaced in September 1914 by the 1st Devonshire Regt.)

*9th Infantry Brigade*
1st Northumberland Fusiliers
4th Royal Fusiliers
1st Lincolnshire Regt.
1st Royal Scots Fusiliers
plus Artillery and Divisional Troops including 'C' Squadron 15th Hussars and the 3rd Cyclist Company

### 5th Division
GOC: Major-General Sir C. Fergusson

*13th Infantry Brigade*
2nd King's Own Scottish Borderers
2nd Duke of Wellington's (West Riding) Regt.
1st The Queen's Own (Royal West Kent) Regt.
2nd King's Own Yorkshire Light Infantry

*14th Infantry Brigade*
2nd Suffolk Regt.
1st East Surrey Regt.
1st Duke of Cornwall' Light Infantry
2nd Manchester Regt.

*15th Infantry Brigade*
1st Norfolk Regt.
1st Bedfordshire Regt.
1st Cheshire Regt.
plus Artillery and Divisional Troops including the 'A' Squadron 19th Hussars and the 5th Cyclist Company.

## THIRD CORPS
*Formed in France on 31 August 1914*

GOC: Major-General W. P. Pulteney

### 4th Division (landed in France 22/23 August 1914)
GOC: Major-General T. D. O'Snow

*10th Infantry Brigade*
1st Royal Warwickshire Regt.
2nd Seaforth Highlanders
1st Royal Irish Fusiliers
2nd Royal Dublin Fusiliers

*11th Infantry Division*
1st Somerset Light Infantry
1st East Lancashire Regt
1st Rifle Brigade

*12th Infantry Brigade*
1st King's Own Royal Lancaster Regt.
2nd Lancashire Fusiliers
2nd Royal Inniskilling Fusiliers
2nd Essex Regt.

lus Artillery and Divisional Troops including 'B' quadron 19th Hussars and the 4th Cyclist Company.

**th Division** (landed in France 9/10 September 1914)
*GOC*: Major-General J. L. Keir

| *6th Infantry Brigade* | *17th Infantry Brigade* |
|---|---|
| st East Kent Regt. (The Buffs) | 1st Royal Fusiliers |
| st Leicestershire Regt. | 1st North Staffordshire Regt. |
| st King's Shropshire Light Infantry | 2nd Leinster Regt. (Royal Canadians) |
| nd Yorks and Lancs Regt. | 3rd Rifle Brigade |

*8th Infantry Brigade*
st West Yorkshire Regt.
st East Yorkshire Regt.
nd Nottinghamshire and Derbyshire Regt. (Sherwood Foresters)
nd Durham Light Infantry

lus Artillery and Divisional Troops including 'C' quadron 19th Hussars, and the 6th Cyclist Company.

Army troops included 'A' and 'C' Squadrons of the orth Irish Horse and 'B' Squadron of the South Irish orse; the 1st Battalion Cameron Highlanders; Siege rtillery; three Signal Companies; five RE Air-Line Sections and eleven Cable Sections plus a Wireless Section.

The force included 2nd, 3rd, 4th, 5th and 6th Aeroplane Squadrons of the Royal Flying Corps commanded by Brigadier-General Sir D. Henderson.

The Line of Communication Defence Battalions were: 1st Devonshire Regt., 2nd Royal Welsh Fusiliers*, 1st Cameronians*, 1st Middlesex Regt.*, and 2nd Argyll and Sutherland Highlanders*. The Line of Communications troops included RE; Signal Service; Medical; Ordnance; Veterinary; Pay; Postal, and Provost units, the latter responsible for setting up military prisons.

*These four battalions were formed into the 19th Infantry Brigade at Valenciennes on 22 August 1914.

# BRITISH FORCES IN ITALY
## NOVEMBER–DECEMBER 1917

*Commander in Chief*: General Sir Herbert Plumer

*The Eleventh Corps arrived in Italy in December 1917 and was commanded by Lieutenant-General Sir Richard Haking.*

*Corps Troops* included 1/1st King Edward's Horse; HQ Corps Heavy Artillery; 11th Cyclist Battalion; Signal Troops; Siege Parks and Ammunition Parks; the 321st ASC Supply Column; 5th Light Ordnance Mobile Workshop; and the 491st ASC Coy. attached to the Heavy Artillery.

*XIV Corps arrived on 5 November 1917, commanded by Lieutenant-General the Earl of Cavan.*

*Corps Troops* included the 1/1st Northamptonshire Yeomanry; 14th Cyclist Battalion; and a similar structure to the Eleventh Corps as described.

**5th Division** (arrived on 27 November 1917 and left Italy for the Western Front between 1 and 9 April 1918)

*GOC*: Major-General R. B. Stephens

*Divisional Troops* included two Brigades of RFA; three Trench Mortar Batteries; a Divisional Ammunition Column; three Field Companies RE; a Signal Company; the 1/6th Argyll and Sutherland Highlanders (Pioneer Battalion); the 2/5th Machine Gun Company; four companies of ASC acting as a Train, a Veterinary Section and an Employment Company.

| *13th Brigade* | *15th Brigade* |
|---|---|
| 14th Royal Warwickshire Regt. | 16th Royal Warwickshire Regt. |
| 15th Royal Warwickshire Regt. | 1st Norfolk Regt. |
| 2nd King's Own Scottish Borderers | 1st Bedfordshire Regt. |
| 1st Royal West Kents | 1st Cheshire Regt. |
| 13th Machine Gun Company | 15th Machine Gun Company |
| 13th Trench Mortar Battery | 15th Trench Mortar Battery |

*95th Brigade*
1st Devonshire Regt.
12th Gloucester Regt.
1st East Surreys
1st Duke of Cornwall's Light Infantry
95th Machine Gun Battery
95th Trench Mortar Battery

**7th Division** (arrived on 17 November 1917)

*GOC*: Major-General T. H. Shoubridge

*Divisional Troops* structure was similar to that described for the 5th Division.

*20th Brigade*

| | |
|---|---|
| 8th Devonshire Regt. | 20th Machine Gun Company |
| 9th Devonshire Regt. | 20th Trench Mortar Battery |
| 2nd Border Regt. | |
| 2nd Gordon Highlanders | |

| *22nd Brigade* | |
|---|---|
| 2nd Royal Warwickshire Regt. | Artillery Company |
| 1st Royal Welch Fusiliers | 22nd Machine Gun Company |
| 20th Manchester Regt. | 22nd Trench Mortar Battery |
| 2nd/1st Honourable | |

*91st Brigade*
2nd Queen's Regt.
1st South Staffordshire Regt.
21st Manchester Regt.
22nd Manchester Regt.
91st Machine Gun Company
91st Trench Mortar Battery

**23rd Division** (arrived during the period 6 to 1 November 1917 and remained in Italy until the troop were demobilised in March 1919)

*GOC*: Major-General Sir J. M. Babington

*Divisional Troops* structure as for the 5th Division. The Pioneer Battalion was the 9th South Staffordshire Regiment.

| *68th Brigade* | *69th Brigade* |
|---|---|
| 10th Northumberland Fusiliers | 11th West Yorkshire Regt. |
| 11th Northumberland Fusiliers | 8th Green Howards |
| 12th Durham Light Infantry | 9th Green Howards |
| 13th Durham Light Infantry | 10th Duke of Wellington's Regt. |
| 68th Machine Gun Company | 69th Machine Gun Company |
| 68th Trench Mortar Battery | 69th Trench Mortar Battery |

*70th Brigade*
11th Sherwood Foresters
8th King's Own Yorkshire Light Infantry
9th Yorks and Lancs Regt.
70th Machine Gun Company
70th Trench Mortar Battery

**41st Division** (arrived in Italy on 16 November 1917, and returned to France in March 1918)

*GOC*: Major-General Sir S. T. B. Lawford

*Divisional Troops* as 5th Division; the 19th Battalion Middlesex Regiment was the Pioneer Battalion.

| *122nd Brigade* | *123rd Brigade* |
|---|---|
| 12th East Surreys | 11th Queen's Regt. |
| 15th Hampshire Regt. (Hampshire Carbineers) | 10th Royal West Kents |
| | 23rd Middlesex Regt. |
| 11th Royal West Kents | 20th Durham Light Infantry |
| 18th KRRC | 123rd Machine Gun Company |
| 122nd Machine Gun Company | 123rd Trench Mortar Battery |
| 122nd Trench Mortar Company | |

Helmet of a Grenadier Guards officer; it has a tailor-made, fine khaki serge cover bearing an unofficial regimental 'flash' of blue and crimson ribbon with a gold-embroidered regimental badge on black backing superimposed. Note the leather chinstrap. (Courtesy Officer Commanding Grenadier Guards)

Men of the Leicestershire Regiment near Contalmaison, July 1916, caught by the camera in a moment of unselfconscious humanity behind the fighting line. This photograph clearly illustrates the fighting garb of the British infantryman. Note the length of the bayonet, and the wire-cutters attached to the rifle. The entrenching tool helve attached to the bayonet scabbard is clearly visible here; note also the canvas case for the early Phenate-Hexane helmet gas-mask slung just behind the scabbard. (IWM)

*124th Brigade*
10th Queen's Regt.
26th Royal Fusiliers
32nd Royal Fusiliers
21st KRRC
124th Machine Gun Company
124th Trench Mortar Battery

**48th (South Midlands) Division** (arrived in Italy on 22 November 1917 and remained until demobilised on 31 March 1919; re-formed in the UK in 1920)

*GOC*: Major-General R. Fanshawe
*Divisional Troops* substantially the same as for the 5th Division. The 1/5th Royal Sussex Regt. was the Pioneer element.

| *143rd (Warwickshire) Brigade* | *144th (Gloucester and Worcestershire) Brigade* |
|---|---|
| 1/5th, 1/6th, 1/7th, and 1/8th Royal Warwickshire Regt. | 1/4th and 1/6th Gloucestershire Regt. |
| 143rd Machine Gun Company | 1/7th and 1/8th Worcestershire Regt. |
| 143rd Trench Mortar Battery | 144th Machine Gun Company |
| | 144th Trench Mortar Battery RA |

**The crew of an 18-pdr gun in action on the Sturma front, 1916. They wear trench caps, and puttees tied cavalry fashion. The figure in the foreground manning the gun trail wears the 90-round cavalry bandolier instead of the normal 50-round version worn by the Royal Artillery and the remainder of the crew. (IWM)**

*145th (South Midland) Brigade*
1/5th Gloucestershire Regt.
1/4th Oxs and Bucks Light Infantry
1/4th Royal Berkshire Regt.
145th Machine Gun Company
145th Trench Mortar Battery RA

In June 1918 the British Forces in Italy were commanded by General the Earl of Cavan.

## MESOPOTAMIA
### INDIAN EXPEDITIONARY FORCE 'D'

Commanded initially by Lieutenant-General Sir A. A. Barrett, it comprised three brigades in November 1914. These, the 16th (Poona), 17th (Ahmednagar) and 18th (Begaum) each had one battalion of British infantry—2nd Dorsetshire Regiment, 1st Oxfordshire and Buckinghamshire Light Infantry, and 2nd Norfolk Regiments respectively—and the remaining infantry were Indian. Divisional troops included some British RFA batteries but remainder were Indian Mountain Batteries, Cavalry.

The Order of Battle for April 1915 indicates command had passed to General Sir John Nixon. There were then two divisions, the 6th and 12th. The former was commanded by Major-General C. Townsend and comprised the 16th, 17th and 18th Brigades, the latter by Major-General G. Gorringe and contained the 12th,

30th and 33rd Brigades. Army Troops comprised the 5th Cavalry Brigade, four Indian regiments and the 10th RFA Brigade and 1st Heavy Brigade RA. Remaining support troops were Indian.

## GALLIPOLI
### ORIGINAL ORDER OF BATTLE

*Commanded by General Sir Ian Hamilton*

**29th Division**
GOC: Major-General A. G. Hunter-Weston

*86th Infantry Brigade*
2nd Royal Fusiliers
1st Lancashire Fusiliers
1st Royal Munster
  Fusiliers
1st Royal Dublin Fusiliers

*87th Infantry Brigade*
2nd South Wales
  Borderers
1st King's Own Scottish
  Borderers
1st Royal Inniskilling
  Fusiliers
1st Border Regt.

*88th Infantry Brigade*
4th Worcestershire Regt.
2nd Hampshire Regt.
1st Essex Regt.
5th Royal Scots (TA)

There was in addition the *Anzac Army Corps* commanded by Lieutenant-General Sir W. R. Birdwood, which comprised the *Australian Division* and the *Australian/New Zealand Division* (mounted units left their horses in Egypt), and a French expeditionary force. The Indian Brigade was left in Egypt until 1 May. Total force: 70,000 officers and men.

## EGYPTIAN EXPEDITIONARY FORCE

*Commander-in-Chief*: General Sir E. H. H. Allenby
The following précis of the Order of Battle omits reference to Australian, Indian, West Indian, French and Italian contingents who formed part of the force, or to the Arab Army and large Egyptian Labour Force.
*General HQ Troops*
South Nottinghamshire Hussars
Two batteries RGA
Two Light Armoured Car Batteries, Machine Gun
  Corps
Variety of RE and Signal Service companies and ASC
  support columns
38th and 39th Battalions Royal Fusiliers

## EASTERN FORCE

## THE DESERT COLUMN

This became the Desert Mounted Corps in August 1917. Commanded by Major-General H. G. Chauvel, it included the 1/1st Worcestershire Yeomanry detached from XX Corps; the 1st, 2nd, 3rd, 4th and 8th Light

Armoured Car Patrols of the Machine Gun Corps; and a variety of RE, Signal Service, ASC, and Ordnance support units.

## XX CORPS

GOC: Lieutenant-General Sir William Chetwode
*HQ Mounted Troop*: 1/1st Worcestershire Yeomanry

## XXI CORPS

GOC: Lieutenant-General Sir Edward Bulfin
*HQ Mounted Troop*: A composite force of 'A' Squadron of the Duke of Lancs Own Yeomanry, and 'A' and 'B' Squadrons of the 1/1st Herts Yeomanry.

**Chaytor's Force**

Operating between 19 September and 31 October 1918, this was commanded by Major-General Sir E. W. C. Chaytor, and comprised 38th and 39th Battalions Royal Fusiliers.

**4th Cavalry Division** (earlier known as the *1st Mounted Division*, later the *Yeomanry Mounted Division*)
GOC: Major-General Sir G. de S. Barrow

*10th Cavalry Brigade*
1/1st Dorset Yeomanry
1/1st Bucks Yeomanry
1/1st Berks Yeomanry
10th Cavalry Brigade
  Signal Troop and 17th
  Machine Gun
  Squadron

*11th Cavalry Brigade*
1/1st County of London
  Yeomanry
1/1st City of London
  Yeomanry
1/3rd County of London
  Yeomanry
11th Cavalry Brigade
  Signal Troop and
  21st Machine Gun
  Squadron

*12th Cavalry Brigade*
1/1st Staffordshire Yeomanry
1/1st Lincolnshire Yeomanry
1/1st East Riding Yeomanry
12th Cavalry Brigade Signal Troop and 18th
  Machine Gun Squadron
*Corps Cavalry Regiment*: 1/2nd County of London Yeomanry

The Yeomanry Regiments of which this division was formed left England in 1915 and served as detachments, brigades and regiments on the Egyptian, Gallipoli and Salonika fronts. As part of the Desert Column they took part in the advance from the Suez Canal, participating in the battle of Gaza in March and April 1917. Six regiments were withdrawn in 1918 to serve as machine gunners on the Western Front, the vacancies being filled by Indian units.

Trooper of Northamptonshire Yeomanry, wearing full marching order. The helmet has a cover with a rolled neck-curtain, and the regimental badge fastened to the front. The canvas feed-bag, picketing peg and rope, canvas water bucket, shoecase and sword worn on the nearside of the saddle are clearly visible, as is the extra bandolier worn round the horse's neck. (IWM)

## 5th Cavalry Division

*GOC*: Major-General H. J. M. MacAndrew

*13th Cavalry Brigade*
1/1st Warwickshire
   Yeomanry
1/1st Gloucestershire
   Yeomanry
13th Cavalry Brigade
   Signal Troop and
   19th Machine Gun
   Squadron

*14th Cavalry Brigade*
1/1st Sherwood Rangers
14th Cavalry Brigade
   Signal Troop and
   20th Machine Gun
   Squadron

The 15th Cavalry Brigade was entirely composed of Indian regiments. The 5th Cavalry Division served initially in France; landing in Egypt in March 1918, it joined the Desert Column on 2 July.

## 3rd (Lahore) Division

*GOC*: Major-General A. R. Hoskins

*7th Infantry Brigade*
1st Connaught Rangers
7th Light Trench Mortar
   Battery

*8th Infantry Brigade*
1st Manchester Regt.
8th Light Trench Mortar
   Battery

*9th Infantry Brigade*
2nd Dorsetshire Regt.
9th Light Trench Mortar Battery

*Divisional Troops* included 7th, 14th and 69th, 372nd, 373rd, 428th, 66th, 374th and 430th Batteries RFA; 65th Field Company RE; 3rd Divisional Signal Company RE and the 131st, 132nd and 133rd Companies of the 3rd Divisional Machine Gun Battalion. The Lahore Division served on the Western Front in 1914 and 1915, in Mesopotamia in 1916 and 1917, and joined XXI Corps in June 1918, relieving the 54th Division in the line on a front of eight miles.

## 7th (Indian) Division

*GOC*: Major-General Sir V. B. Fane

*19th Infantry Brigade*
1st Seaforth Highlanders
19th Trench Mortar
   Battery

*21st Infantry Brigade*
2nd Black Watch
21st Light Trench Mortar
   Battery

*28th Infantry Brigade*
2nd Leicestershire Regt.
28th Light Trench Mortar Battery

*Divisional Troops* included five RFA Brigades, some transferred from the 52nd (Lowland) Division; the 522nd London Field Company RE; and three companies of the Machine Gun Corps. The 7th (Indian) Division served initially in France, then in Mesopotamia, and landed in Egypt in January 1918 to relieve the 54th Division in the coastal area of the front line. The Divisional Artillery of the 52nd Division were taken over by the 7th when the 52nd returned to France.

## 10th Division

*GOC*: Major-General J. R. Longley

*29th Infantry Brigade*
1st Leinster Regt.
5th Connaught Rangers
6th Leinster Regt.
6th Royal Irish Rifles
29th Light Trench
   Mortar Battery

*30th Infantry Brigade*
2nd Royal Irish Fusiliers
5th and 6th Royal
   Inniskilling Fusiliers
31st Light Trench Mortar
   Battery

Divisional Artillery included three Brigades RFA and three companies of the Machine Gun Corps. The 10th (Irish) Division was originally composed of 'New Army' Battalions of Irish Regiments. It saw service at Gallipoli and in Salonika, and landed in Egypt September 1917. In May and June 1918 the 'New Army' Battalions were withdrawn and returned to France and their places filled by Indian units.

## 52nd (Lowland) Division

*GOC*: Major-General W. E. B. Smith

*155th Infantry Brigade*
1/4th and 1/5th Royal
   Scots Fusiliers
1/4th and 1/5th King's
   Own Scottish
   Borderers
155th Machine Gun
   Battery
155th Light Trench
   Mortar Battery

*156th Infantry Brigade*
1/4th and 1/7th
   Battalions Royal Scots
1/7th and 1/8th Scottish
   Rifles
156th Machine Gun
   Battery
156th Light Trench
   Mortar Battery

1 Bomber, 10th Bn. Cameronians, 15th Division, 1915
2 2nd Lt., 6th Bn., South Wales Borderers, 30th Div., 1915
3 Private, 2nd Bn., Black Watch, December 1914

G. A. EMBLETON

A

B

G. A. EMBLETO

1 **Sergeant, 17th Lancers, 1918**
2 **Trooper, Dorset Yeomanry**
3 **Sergeant, Queen's Oxfordshire Hussars**

G. A. EMBLETON

C

1 2nd Lt., London Scottish, 168th Bde., 56th Div., Somme 1916
2 Sergeant, 1st Bn., Lancashire Fusiliers, 29th Div., Somme 1916
3 Infantry in winter trench order, 1916/17

D

G. A. EMBLETO

1 **Major, 1/6th Bn., Royal Welsh Fusiliers, 158th Bde., 53rd Div., Palestine 1917**
2 **Lieutenant, 5th Bn., Hampshire Regt., 75th Div., Palestine 1917**
3 **Private, 6th (Pioneer) Bn., East Yorks. Regt., 42nd Div., Gallipoli 1915**
4 **Private, 1/5th Bn., Essex Regt., 163rd Bde., 54th Div., Palestine 1917**

A. EMBLETON

E

1 Private, 1/4th Bn., Royal Sussex Regt., 160th Bde., 53rd Div.,
Sinai 1916/17
2 Sergeant, 12th Bn., Argyll & Sutherland Highlanders, 65th Bde.,
22nd Div., Salonika 1916
3 Sergeant, 1st Bn., Suffolk Regt., 84th Bde., 28th Div., Macedonia 1916
4 Trooper, 25th Bn., Royal Welsh Fusiliers, Palestine 1917

F

1 Private, 'A' Bn., Tank Corps, France 1917
2 Driver, Royal Field Artillery, 51st Div., France 1917

A. EMBLETON

G

## 157th Infantry Brigade
1/5th, 1/6th and 1/7th Highland Light Infantry
1/5th Argyll and Sutherland Highlanders
157th Machine Gun Battery
157th Light Trench Mortar Battery

*Divisional Troops* included the 52nd Division Cyclist Company, three Brigades RFA which were later transferred to the 7th Indian Division, the Pioneer Battalion of the 5th Royal Irish Regiment, the 211th Machine Gun Company, two Trench Mortar Batteries RA, three Field Companies RE. The 52nd Division, composed entirely of Lowland Territorial battalions served with distinction through the Gallipoli campaign and took part in the advance across the desert from Sinai. It took part in the final overthrow of the Turks in actions at Gaza and the subsequent advances, but returned to France in April 1918.

## 53rd Division
GOC: Major-General S. F. Mott

*158th Infantry Brigade*
5/6th Royal Welsh Fusiliers (1/5th and 1/6th amalgamating in August 1918)
1/1st Herefordshire Regt.
158th Light Trench Mortar Battery

*159th Infantry Brigade*
4/5th Welch Regt. (1/4th and 1/5th amalgamating August 1918)
1/4th and 1/7th Cheshire Regt.
159th Light Trench Mortar Battery

*160th Infantry Brigade*
1/7th Royal Welsh Fusiliers
2/4th Royal West Kent Regt.
2/10th Middlesex Regt.
2/4th Queen's Royal West Surrey Regt.
1/4th Royal Sussex Regt.
160th Light Trench Mortar Battery

*Divisional Troops* included 53rd Division Cyclist Company; three Brigades RFA; two Field Companies RE; 53rd Divisional Machine Gun Battalion, and the 155th Indian Pioneer Battalion. Composed originally of Territorial battalions, the division served in Gallipoli before going to Egypt. It took part in the battles of Gaza, and was eventually pulled out of the line for re-organisation on joining XXI Corps.

## 54th (East Anglian) Division
GOC: Major-General S. W. Hare

*161st Infantry Brigade*
1/4th, 1/5th, 1/6th and 1/7th Battalions Essex Regt.
161st Light Trench Mortar Battery
*162nd Infantry Brigade*
1/5th Bedfordshire Regt.
1/4th Northamptonshire Regt.
1/10th and 1/11th London Regt.
162nd Light Trench Mortar Battery
*163rd Infantry Brigade*
1/4th and 1/5th Norfolk Regt.

1/5th Suffolk Regt.
1/8th Hampshire Regt.
163rd Light Trench Mortar Battery

*Divisional Troops* included three Brigades RFA; three Field Companies RE; and the 54th Division Machine Gun Battalion. This division was composed entirely of Territorial battalions. It fought through the Gallipoli campaign; landed in Egypt December 1915, marched across the desert from the Suez Canal, and took part in the battles of Gaza. Throughout the Palestine campaign this division fought without change in its order of battle.

## 60th Division
GOC: Major-General E. S. Bulfin

*179th Infantry Brigade*
2/13th, 1/14th, 2/15th and 2/16th London Regt.
179th Light Trench Mortar Battery

*180th Infantry Brigade*
2/17th, 2/18th, 2/19th and 2/20th London Regt. (2/18th disbanded 10 July 1918)
180th Trench Mortar Battery

*181st Infantry Brigade*
2/21st, 2/22nd, 2/23rd, 2/24th London Regt.
181st Light Trench Mortar Battery

*Divisional Troops* included three Brigades RFA; two Field Companies RE; and the 60th Divisional Machine Gun Battalion. The 60th was a London division composed entirely of Territorial battalions. It served in France from June to December 1916, was then transferred to Salonika, and eventually went to Egypt in June 1917. It reached the front in July and joined XX Corps in August. Reorganised in July 1918, it had seven of the best battalions withdrawn for service in France; two were disbanded. The vacancies were filled by Indian units and the London TA title was then dropped.

## 74th (Yeomanry) Division
GOC: Major-General E. S. Girdwood

*229th Infantry Brigade*
16th (Royal 1st Devon & Royal North Devon Yeomanry) Bn., Devonshire Regt.
12th (West Somerset Yeomanry) Bn., Somerset Light Infantry
14th (Fife & Forfar Yeomanry) Bn., Black Watch
12th (Ayr & Lanark Yeomanry) Bn., Royal Scots Fusiliers
4th Machine Gun Company
229th Light Trench Mortar Battery
*230th Infantry Brigade*
10th (Royal East Kent & West Kent Yeomanry) Bn., East Kent Regt.
16th (Sussex Yeomanry) Bn., Royal Sussex Regt.
15th (Suffolk Yeomanry) Bn., Suffolk Regt.
12th (Norfolk Yeomanry) Bn., Norfolk Regt.
209th Machine Gun Company
230th Light Trench Mortar Battery

*231st Infantry Brigade*
10th (Shropshire & Cheshire Yeomanry) Bn., King's
   Shropshire Light Infantry
24th (Denbighshire Yeomanry) Bn., Royal Welsh
   Fusiliers
25th (Montgomeryshire & Welsh Horse Yeomanry)
   Bn., Welch Regt.
24th (Pembroke & Glamorgan Yeomanry) Bn., Welch
   Regt.
210th Machine Gun Company
231st Trench Mortar Battery

*Divisional Troops* included two Brigades RFA; three Field Companies RE; the 1/12th Pioneer Battalion of the Loyal North Lancashire Regiment; and the 261st Machine Gun Company. Formed in 1917, this Yeomanry Division included twelve dismounted regiments which had fought in Gallipoli. Battalions were brought up to strength by drafts, and reached the front in time to take part in the second battle of Gaza. It joined XX Corps in August, held parts of the line and aided in constructing new defences on the left sector until March 1918, when it returned to France.

## 74th Division
      *GOC*: Major-General P. C. Palin

| | |
|---|---|
| *232nd Infantry Brigade* | *233rd Infantry Brigade* |
| 1/4th Wiltshire Regt. | 1/5th Somerset Light |
| 2/5th Hampshire Regt. |    Infantry |
| 2/4th Somerset Light | 2/4th Dorset Regt. |
|    Infantry | 2/4th Hampshire Regt. |
| 1/5th Devonshire Regt. | 233rd Light Trench |
| 232nd Light Trench |    Mortar Battery |
|    Mortar Battery | |

*234th Infantry Brigade*
1/4th Duke of Cornwall Light Infantry
2/4th Devonshire Regt.
234th Light Trench Mortar Battery

*Divisional Troops* included two Brigades RFA; one Field Company RE; and 75th Divisional Machine Gun Battalion. The division comprised Territorial and Indian units recently arrived from India. Included in XXI Corps, it began operations in October 1917. It served in the Sinai and Palestine areas until the end of the war.

## The Imperial Camel Corps Brigade
Commanded by Brigadier-General C. L. Smith, VC, MC, this was a mixture of Anzac and British. The second battalion comprised four British companies with two detached independent British companies. The 26th Machine Gun Squadron was formed from the Scottish Horse.

The Palestine Lines of Communication comprised mixed Anzac, British, and Indian forces. Mounted troops included 'C' Squadron of the Glasgow Yeomanry, less one troop. Infantry included the 1st (Garrison)

Battalions of the Royal Warwickshire Regiment; Devonshire Regiment; Essex Regiment; Northamptonshire Regiment; Cheshire Regiment; and the 19th (Western) Battalion of the Rifle Brigade.

In Egypt was one British company of the Imperial Camel Corps, one troop of 'C' Squadron the Glasgow Yeomanry, plus the 1st (Garrison) Battalions the Notts and Derby Regiment and the Royal Irish Regiment, the 2nd (G) Battalion the Royal Welsh Fusiliers, 20th (G) Battalion of the Rifle Brigade, 40th (Palestinian) Battalion of the Royal Fusiliers, plus an Armoured Car Brigade and an Armoured Train. At Alexandria was the 1st (Garrison) Battalion the Royal Scots and the 5th (Reserve) Battalion the British West India Regiment.

Each Brigade had a Field Ambulance plus casualty clearing stations, clearing hospitals, medical stores depots, laboratories, sanitary units, hospital trains and barge, general, detention, prisoner of war, and convalescence hospitals.

In 1918 XX Corps were estimated to have 13,200 camels on strength, and XXI Corps had 6,000. The Desert Mounted Corps had a further 1,200, and 2,500 were being used regularly on the lines of communication. By the commencement of operations in September 1918 the strength of both Corps in camels was 25,700. The force had 2,000 donkeys allotted to units in the field formed by the ASC into DTC (Donkey Transport Companies). Twenty thousand Arab drivers were found for the camel transport, and nearly 2,000 more for the donkey units.

# The Plates

*A Infantry 1914–15*
During the last decades of Victoria's reign the army fought many colonial wars, often in hot climates, and during this period experience was gained in the search for a comfortable, inconspicuous field service uniform. This led to the introduction of a khaki uniform in January 1902 which, with few minor changes, was worn until the introduction of 'battledress' in 1937. It included a flat-topped khaki cap (issued in 1909) with a cloth peak and leather chinstrap. As issued the cap had a circular wire stiffener inserted in the crown; this was invariably removed on service in the trenches. The cap was gradually replaced by a more suitable 'trench cap' for officers and men, which had a soft top and peak, and ear-flaps.

Soldiers escorting Bulgarian POWs to the rear after the battle of Doiran, August 1916, displaying clearly the infantry dress worn in the Middle East and other hot climates. (IWM)

The single-breasted khaki serge jacket had a stand-and-fall collar, five brass buttons of general service pattern (black horn in Rifle regiments) and cloth shoulder straps. There were patch pockets with box pleats and oblong flaps fastened by brass buttons on the breasts, and larger pockets, without pleats, in the sides of the skirts. The jacket had a plain back with two hip vents, and cloth reinforcements over the shoulders. The only distinctions were a metal regimental badge on the cap, and brass shoulder titles. NCOs wore light drab herringbone-pattern chevrons on both upper sleeves; there were one or two instances of chevrons being worn with a distinct diamond pattern—possibly a regimental distinction. All arms-of-service except Scottish regiments wore the same jacket. The Scottish pattern had rounded skirt fronts to facilitate wearing the sporran. Under the jacket a waistcoat or cardigan could be worn. The khaki trousers were worn with khaki puttees and ankle boots; dismounted troops wound the puttee from ankle to knee.

*A1 Bomber, 10th (Service) Battalion, Cameronians (Scottish Rifles), 15th (Scottish) Division; France, 1915*

The Mills bomb was an effective weapon for trench fighting and clearing dug-outs. Specially trained personnel known as 'bombers' formed part of infantry units, and were sometimes identified by cloth grenade badges on the sleeves. This soldier is dressed and equipped for a trench raid during the early part of the war. He wears a knitted cap in place of the normal headdress. In place of standard webbing pouches he has the special harness for carrying grenades, later to be replaced by canvas bags. He is armed with weapons specially designed for trench fighting and invariably made by the men themselves—a club, and a knife with a knuckle-guard.

*A2 2nd Lieutenant, 6th (Pioneer) Battalion, South Wales Borderers, 30th Division; France, 1915*

Army Order 10, dated 1 January 1902, prescribed the officers' uniform. The jacket was originally to be five-buttoned with a closed collar but was altered to open neck, stepped collar, worn with a tie, before the commencement of hostilities. The Foot Guards never wore tunics with closed collars and, unlike line infantry, always wore rank badges on the shoulder straps. The original shoulder ornaments were narrow plaited cords of khaki and white mixture; rank distinctions comprised a system of vertical braids on the cuffs terminating in trefoils. This system seems to have been little, if ever, used and, in any event, lasted only about six months. It was replaced by the design illustrated here: a system of brown and light drab braid rings with braid-edged three-pointed khaki flaps superimposed, bearing stars and crowns of rank. During the course of the war a method of wearing rank badges on the shoulder straps became accepted, although it was not officially sanctioned until 1922. Riding breeches of Bedford cord were worn with puttees and ankle boots, riding boots, or 'Stohwasser' gaiters. Khaki trousers were also worn with puttees. The original order decreed that officers should wear arm-of-service colours and rank distinctions on the greatcoat shoulder straps; in some regiments this was observed up until the end of the war, and in the Royal Fusiliers until 1945.

This officer wears regimental badges on the cap and collar, and the divisional sign on both upper sleeves. The division was raised as the 37th in 1914, and renumbered as the 30th in 1915. By May of 1918 it had virtually ceased to exist, and was reconstituted in July, going on to take part in the final advance.

Initially officers went into action wearing the full equipment of Sam Browne belt, pistol and sword, but this was soon replaced by adapted '08 pattern webbing with pistols. Officers of Rifle regiments wore black buttons, boots, and leather equipment. Sticks, usually ashplants, were almost universal. This officer carries his steel helmet slung through a shoulder strap, and a rolled waterproof.

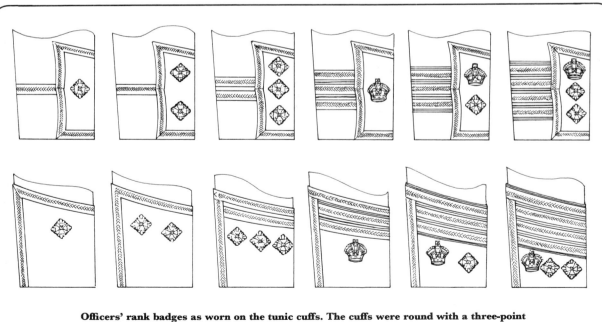

**Officers' rank badges as worn on the tunic cuffs. The cuffs were round with a three-point flap, the flap edged with ½in-wide chevron lace. Badges of rank were in worsted embroidery of light drab—in practical terms, cream-coloured thread. Highland and Lowland Scottish regiments wore a gauntlet cuff laced and embroidered as illustrated in the lower row; the lace began at the top of the cuff, and there was one bar of lace down the back seam. Officers' khaki drill jackets for wear in hot climates had a pointed cuff, and the ranking was worn on the shoulder straps. From left to right, both rows: 2nd Lieutenant, Lieutenant, Captain, Major, Lieutenant-Colonel, Colonel.**

*A3 Private, 2nd Battalion, 42nd Royal Highlanders, The Black Watch; France, December 1914*

Highland regiments wore the kilt with a drill apron. Regimental hose-tops were worn with drill gaiters, later replaced by short khaki puttees. The 2nd Bn. arrived in France from India in October 1914, dressed in tropical clothing. While in a camp at Marseilles this was replaced by khaki serge with a field service cap, in which they wore the red hackle. The cap was soon 'lost' and replaced by 'cap comforters' or Balaclavas. Highland shoes were worn for their first few hours in the trenches, but many men lost the shoes in the glutinous mud and had to fight in stockinged feet. In December, shoes were replaced by boots and puttees. That winter blue bonnets were issued, small in circumference, and worn with khaki covers, complete with the red hackle. Hose-tops were either khaki or Atholl grey, with scarlet garters.

*B1 Captain, The Black Watch; Mounted Divisional Staff, 40th Division; France, 1918*

This 'New Army' division was sent to France in

**14th (King's) Hussars resting on their way back from the third action at Jebel Hamrin. All wear lightweight khaki drill uniforms, Wolseley helmet with pagri and regimental flash, and in some cases a neck-curtain. Note the full marching order carried by the horses, some of which have 'anti-fly fringes' on the brow bands. (IWM)**

1916; it was originally called a 'Bantam Division'—a euphemism for the relaxation of minimum height and other physical requirements for enlistment. After its capture of Bourlon Wood in November 1917 an 'acorn' was added to the diamond-shaped formation sign. It took part in the battles of the Somme, the attack on the Hindenburg Line, Cambrai, St. Quentin, Bapaume, the Lys, Estaires, Nazebruck and Ypres 1918. This Staff Captain wears the Highland pattern service tunic; the regimental Glengarry with the large silver regimental cap badge worn forward on the left side mounted on a black cockade; Government sett tartan breeches; heavy black gaiters, and ankle boots with strapped spurs. His brassard includes the divisional sign with the 'acorn'.

For easy identification of command duties, Staff officers wore $3\frac{1}{2}$in cloth brassards on the sleeve.

Among the most important were:

*GHQ*: Red over black, a black crown on the red, and an identifying initial in red on the black (eg, Q=Quartermaster).

*HQ Home Forces and BEF*: As GHQ but with the initial only, in red on the black (eg, BEF).

*Command HQ*: Red with central black stripe, lettered red (eg, ST=Supply and Transport).

*Corps HQ*: Red with central white stripe, with, on occasion, a corps or divisional sign.

*Divisional HQ*: Red, with black lettering identifying service (eg, O=Ordnance).

*Brigade HQ*: Blue with black lettering (eg, BM=Brigade Major).

*B2 Lieutenant-Colonel, Brigade Staff*

Prior to 1916 the Dress Regulations of 1911 prescribed that substantive colonels and officers on the Staff should wear scarlet gorget patches with a central line of crimson silk gimp. Army Service Corps Staff wore blue patches with a white silk line; Medical Staff colonels, blue patches with black braid lines; and other Medical Staff, plain blue. Ordnance Staff wore blue patches with lines of scarlet braid; Pay Department Staff, blue with $\frac{1}{2}$in wide yellow lines; Veterinary colonels, maroon with a scarlet braid line; other Veterinary Staff, plain maroon; and School of Instruction Inspectors, blue patches with light blue silk lines.

In 1916 Army Order 92 prescribed new distinctions. In future scarlet patches with crimson gimp lines would be worn by Staff captains and lieutenants, besides a list of other appointments. The Chief Paymaster, Chief Engineer, RE Staff, Chief Ordnance Officer, Provost Marshal, Garrison Adjutants, Director of Medical Services, Embarkation Staff, etc., were ordered to wear blue cap bands and blue gorget patches with crimson gimp lines. Recruiting Staff, Intelligence, Musketry Instruction, Catering, Gymnasia and Assistant Directors of Transport, among other miscellaneous appointments, would wear green cap bands and green patches with green gimp lines.

*B3 General Officer*

Field Marshals and General Officers had two rows of gold oakleaf embroidery on their cap peaks; the caps were the blue undress caps, worn with khaki covers and scarlet bands fitted to cover the original design. The tunics had plain cuffs, and the following rank badges were worn on the shoulder straps:

*Field Marshal*: crossed batons on a wreath of laurel with crown above. *General*: crossed mameluke sabre and baton with a crown and star above. *Lieutenant-General*: crossed sabre and baton with crown above. *Major-General*: crossed sabre and baton with a star above. General Officers' cap-badges comprised a crossed sabre and baton within a laurel wreath surmounted by the Royal Crest (crowned lion on crown), all in gold. Generals' gorget patches were scarlet with a line of gold oakleaf embroidery.

Staff officers with the rank of General Officer wore scarlet patches with gold chain gimp lines; similar patches were worn by Staff officers serving on the GHQ staff. The Staff cap-badge was the Royal Crest in gold.

*C Cavalry types*

Cavalry wore standard khaki serge jackets but with cord breeches and puttees, tied at the ankle rather than at the knee as was the case in dismounted units. Accoutrements comprised a leather 1903 pattern cartridge bandolier holding up to ninety rounds in five front and four back pouches. The waterbottle and haversack were worn slung over the right shoulder, high under the left arm. Personal weapons consisted of the standard .303 SMLE rifle carried in a 'bucket' on the saddle, and the 1908 pattern sword carried in a frog on the saddle. Lances were seldom, if ever used in action, but were carried by General Officers' mounted orderlies. In lieu of the rifle, warrant officers, staff sergeants and sergeants were supposed to carry a holstered pistol with lanyard, and ammunition pouch with twelve rounds, on a brown leather waistbelt.

Horse furniture comprised a brown leather headstall, bridle, saddle, and reins; rifle bucket; sword frog; headrope; set of spare horse shoes; a horse 'rubber'; heel rope; picketing rope and peg; surcingle pad; brush; feed bag, and corn bag. Extra ropes and pegs were issued to men with restive horses. On the front of the saddle were two brown leather wallets for personal effects; over these were strapped a spare pair of boots, with tent canvas strapped overall. At the rear of the saddle the rider strapped his greatcoat—the short version known as

Two members of the Royal Engineers with one of the many types of vehicle used by this versatile corps—a steam traction engine. (D. Fosten)

Both these sergeants of artillery wear the stiff cap and standard khaki jacket, but, interestingly, they have cord riding breeches. The seated NCO has 'dispatch rider' boots with spurs, and the standing man, leather gaiters and spurs. They seem to be wearing cap covers, and both have whistles on the right breast pockets. Both wear an unusual badge superimposed on the chevrons on both arms—unfortunately the details are not clear. The seated figure has three overseas service stripes on his lower right sleeve. (Courtesy R. G. Harris)

1st Bn. Royal Irish Regiment on the march in Mesopotamia, June 1916. Note the regimental badges pinned to the left side of the slouch hats. (IWM)

Clyno/Vickers motorcycle and machine gun combination, typical of various combinations used from 1914 onwards in support of, or in place of, mounted cavalry; as the war progressed they were used more and more as machine gun carriers. The gun was not intended to be fired from the sidecar, but from the normal tripod mount which was stowed behind the seat. By 1918 there were some 1,800 Clyno/Vickers combinations in service.

a 'British warm'; a blanket; and a waterproof sheet overall. An extra bandolier with thirty rounds was worn around the horse's neck.

### C1 Sergeant, 17th Lancers, marching order; France, 1918

The regimental badge is painted on the helmet (an unauthorized embellishment); it appears on the collar in brass, an economy practised by many regiments, although it should have been in white metal. In its proper colour it is repeated over the rank chevrons on the right sleeve, a distinction of cavalry NCOs. The *fleur-de-lys* badge in brass identifies a scout. On the right lower sleeve are four small chevrons denoting length of service: one blue for each year's service overseas, and the bottom one red, denoting overseas service in 1914. On the left lower sleeve appear the marksman's distinction of crossed brass rifles, over a gold wound stripe.

### C2 Trooper, Dorset Yeomanry, marching order

This regiment served in the 10th Brigade of the 4th (Yeomanry) Mounted Division in the Middle East, and formed part of the Egyptian Expeditionary Force. A second-line regiment, it was later converted to a cyclist battalion manning coastal defences in Britain. Although retaining cavalry breeches this trooper has no spurs, and is equipped as an infantryman. The green cap band was a regimental distinction.

### C3 Sergeant, The Queen's Oxfordshire Hussars

This Yeomanry regiment served in France. A regimental distinction was that NCOs wore silver badges, buttons and chevrons. In the background, a military policeman escorts a German prisoner.

### D1 2nd Lieutenant, London Scottish (14th County of London Bn. TA); Somme, 1916

When this regiment mobilised in August 1914 they wore regulation marching order. Bonnet badges, sporran badges and tassels were removed before they first went into action at Messines in November 1914. In the spring of 1915 a khaki tam-o'-shanter was issued to replace the blue Glengarry bonnet, but officers continued to wear the latter until 1917, when the two bonnets were worn indiscriminately. Scottish officers wore a special pattern of jacket cut away in front to permit the sporran to be worn; it had gauntlet cuffs edged with rank-ring braid. The regimental tartan was plain 'Hodden Grey', a distinctive grey-mauve heather shade, and hose-tops were the same colour except for pipers and drummers, who retained diced hose-tops.

The steel helmet was issued in 1916, the Somme being the first major action for which all troops received it. Before that the numbers available were limited, and helmets were passed by men leaving the firing line to those relieving them in the trenches. They were generally covered with canvas or hessian to prevent reflection of light. Often they were decorated with regimental, brigade or divisional insignia. Officers of this regiment wore bright blue touries on the left side of the helmet for a while in 1916, but the practice was short-lived.

This officer wears the red triangular sign of 168th Brigade on both sleeves. This brigade was part of 56th (London) Territorial Division, whose device was the red sword of Wat Tyler, point uppermost. It may possibly have been worn on the back of the jacket below the collar. Regimental collar badges are worn, and above the left breast pocket is the ribbon of the Territorial Decoration.

*D2 Sergeant, 1st Battalion, Lancashire Fusiliers, 29th Division; Somme, 1916*

This NCO wears the standard khaki field service dress and steel helmet. The yellow flash on the latter simulates the plume worn in the regimental full dress headdress. The brass shoulder titles are pinned to the outer end of the shoulder straps, and a red formation sign is sewn above the chevrons of rank, half of the 29th Division's red diamond being worn on each sleeve—an unusual way of displaying a divisional sign.

The 1908 Pattern Web Equipment owed its birth to an American officer of the 1880s, Captain Anson Mills, who patented a method of carrying brass cartridges in a webbing belt which avoided the problems associated with leather belts; these 'sweated' in service, and corrosion tended to jam the brass cartridges in their loops. Samples brought to Britain impressed the Quartermaster-General, and a large number were issued to the British army during the late stages of the Boer War. A small factory was set up in London to experiment with the canvas web material, and from it a new pattern of military equipment emerged, culminating in the

Basic army saddle and bridle displayed to good effect by mounted despatch rider, Army Signals, Royal Engineers. (R. Marrion)

'Mills 1908 Pattern Web Infantry Equipment' worn by British infantry until 1937, and in isolated instances, until 1941.

The equipment comprised a 3in-wide waistbelt, a pair of 2in-wide braces, and two cartridge carriers each with five pouches holding a total of 150 rounds. A haversack was carried on the left side of the belt, and suspended from the belt beneath it were the bayonet scabbard and entrenching tool

Despatch riders of Army Signals, Royal Engineers. Two wear the special issue waterproof mackintosh coat; the others can be seen to wear blue and white signals brassards on both sleeves. Despatch riders were issued with leather gaiters or high boots in place of the ankle boots and puttees. (R. Marrion)

handle. The entrenching tool blade was kept in a carrier slung from the belt in the small of the back, and the waterbottle in its web 'cradle' was slung on the right side of the belt. A large knapsack with supporting straps was worn on the back. This equipment proved so successful that many countries experimented with it, including even Germany (although in the event Germany retained leather equipment until 1943–44), and many alternative patterns were produced.

### D3 Soldiers in trench order, winter 1916–17

Conditions in the trenches of the Western Front proved so appalling that many supplementary items had to be provided to make life tolerable. In 1915 goatskin coats, with and without sleeves and cut to different lengths, were issued to men on tour in the front lines. The foul, muddy conditions caused foot disorders collectively termed 'trench feet', and rubber waders and other forms of protective clothing were issued to all ranks. The

ammunition issued to each man was supplemented by cotton bandoliers of 100 rounds worn slung round the shoulders. The three red bars worn at the top of the sleeve are a typical battalion identification.

### E1 Major (Mounted Duties), 1/6th Bn. (TA), Royal Welsh Fusiliers; 158th Brigade, 53rd (Welsh) Division; Palestine, 1917

Initially a pre-war Territorial division, the 53rd adopted the Prince of Wales's Feathers as its sign. In August 1915 it went to Gallipoli, and in December of that year to Egypt; it took part in the advance from Suez to Gaza. In August 1918 it was reconstituted with some South African and Indian formations and dropped the Territorial designation.

This officer wears the drill version of the service dress tunic. Regimental collar badges were not worn with this uniform, and were replaced by shoulder titles. Rank badges are also worn on the shoulder straps by this major. The white plume on the left side of the sun helmet was a short-lived addition. A square of black material was worn on the back centre of the pagri, and the regiment's famous 'black flash', a reminder of the queue bag of a previous age, was sewn to the back of the tunic for

Typical infantry Corps of Drums belonging to the 1st Bn., 1st London Regiment, Royal Fusiliers Territorial Force; France, 1917. The divisional sign, the red sword of Wat Tyler, is shown on the left of the board in the foreground. The 56th (London) Division was formed in France in February 1916, and consisted chiefly of Territorial battalions of the London Regiment; its baptism of fire came in the holocaust of 1 July 1916—'the first day of the Somme'. (D. Fosten)

Company Sergeant Major of the Army Service Corps, showing clearly the '02 khaki field service dress and stiff-topped forage cap. (Courtesy J. Woodroff)

*centre*
Infantry private of the 20th Bn., London Regiment, in full marching order. On the lower left sleeve he wears a vertical gold wound stripe. (Courtesy J. Woodroff)

*right*
Typical summer dress of a member of the Machine Gun Corps on the Western Front in 1917. The waistbelt and braces of the 1914 leather equipment are worn with two small leather ammunition pouches on the right side and a .45 Webley in an open leather holster on the left. He wears shortened trousers (to lessen lice infestation), puttees and boots. On the upper left sleeve can just be seen two cloth formation signs. The lower is the 24th Division sign in saltire form, representing crossed machine guns. A single wound stripe is worn at the bottom of the left sleeve, and two overseas service chevrons at the bottom of the right sleeve. (Courtesy J. Woodroff)

all ranks. The black and white sleeve flash was almost certainly a brigade sign.

### E2 Lieutenant, 5th (TA) Battalion, Hampshire Regiment, 75th Division; Palestine, 1917

This division was formed late in the war, in March 1917, from a mixture of Territorial and Regular units with some Indian formations. The 232nd Brigade captured a famous mosque on the heights outside Jerusalem, the Tomb of Samuel; in its native form the name was corrupted by the troops to 'Neby Sawmill'. This action was considered the key to the battle and as a result the division adopted a key as its sign. This officer wears a battalion flash on his helmet. His shirt is blue-grey, matching the colour of those worn by his men, but with an attached collar.

### E3 Private, 6th (Pioneer) Battalion, East Yorks Regiment, 42nd (East Lancs) Division; Gallipoli, 1915

Most troops landed in Gallipoli from the United Kingdom or Western Front in standard khaki serge field service uniform. This soldier would wear pioneer badges on his collar fronts. At a later stage the white 'P' for pioneer was worn without the blue diamond ground. After the battle of the Somme the unit wore the regimental badge stencilled in black on the front of the steel helmet.

### E4 Private, 1/5th (TA) Battalion, Essex Regiment, 163rd Brigade, 54th (East Anglian) Division; Palestine, 1917

This division, mobilised on the outbreak of war, went to the Dardanelles in August 1915 and fought in the Gallipoli campaign. Transferred to the Egyptian Expeditionary Force the following December, it marched across the desert from Suez and fought in the two battles of Gaza in 1917. The black triangle on the light, quilted neck-curtain tied to the steel helmet was the 163rd Brigade sign. White braces with brown leather loops are worn over the shirt, under the webbing, although invisible from this angle. The standard grey-blue shirt is worn with khaki drill shorts, and full webbing is worn in fighting order.

### F1 Private, 1/4th Battalion, Royal Sussex Regiment, 160th Brigade, 53rd Division; Sinai, 1916–17

The soldier is illustrated in marching order. Haswell-Miller notes: 'A blue patch was worn on both sides of the helmet. The large pack is worn and the haversack was discarded—an extra waterbottle was carried in its place. A bivouac pole was carried strapped to the pack . . .'

Army shirts were a medium blue-grey and were collarless. In hot weather they were worn with rolled sleeves and without the serge or drill jacket. The normal headdress was the Wolseley helmet with pagri, or the felt slouch hat. Khaki drill shorts were worn with khaki puttees and ankle boots. Regardless of the climate full web equipment was carried in full marching order. The contents of the large pack were officially:

| | |
|---|---|
| Greatcoat (necessary for the cold nights) | Spare boots, socks and laces |
| Holdall (kitbag) | Drill or serge jacket |
| Waistcoat and cardigan | Comforter |
| Shaving kit | Change of underclothes |
| Towel and soap | |
| Brush and comb | Ground sheet, folded |
| 'Housewife' | under the flap |

In the trenches the pack was removed and left on the firing-step or in the dug-out. The whole equipment, including rifle and full ammunition, weighed about 60lb.

At the beginning of the war Field Service Regulations divided kit and clothing into three categories: (1) Personal clothing, which included boots, caps, service and full dress and fatigue clothes; (2) Public clothing, which included greatcoats, full dress headdress, breeches, spurs, service helmets, leggings, waterproof capes, Highland sporrans, etc.; (3) Necessaries, which included badges, blacking, laces, brushes, buttonsticks, combs, knives, grease tins, gauntlets, worsted gloves, hose-tops, 'housewives', polishing powder, razor, socks, sponges, pipeclay, spoons, etc.

### F2 Sergeant, 12th (Service) Battalion, Argyll and Sutherland Highlanders, 65th Brigade, 22nd Division, Transport Detachment; Salonika, 1916

This 'New Army' division joined the BEF in September 1915, but two months later it transferred to Salonika and remained in that theatre until the Armistice. This NCO wears a uniform which is generally of cavalry style, including the bandolier. A regimental collar badge is pinned to a blue background and worn on the turned-up brim of the slouch hat. On his shoulder strap is a one-inch black slip-on band; these were worn in different colours by divisions of the Salonika Force.

### F3 Sergeant, 1st Battalion, Suffolk Regiment, 84th Brigade, 28th Division; Macedonia, 1916

This division adopted a red strip across the shoulder straps when the need for identification arose; note the interesting blue shoulder straps. The red cut-out castle was adopted by the Suffolks as their regimental sign, stitched to the turned-up hat brim. The curious split trousers were a feature of hot-weather uniform, worn both in the Middle East and on the Western Front. This division, originally entirely of Regular units, was formed in December 1914 and went to France in 1915. Later, Territorial units were brigaded. It was involved in checking the German breakthrough in the second battle of Ypres in 1915, and in November that year went to Salonika, where it remained until the Armistice.

### F4 Trooper, 25th (Montgomery and Welsh Horse Yeomanry) Battalion, Royal Welsh Fusiliers; Palestine, 1917

This trooper in marching order wears the 1914 leather equipment, including an '03 pattern bandolier. Officers of this unit also wore an additional sign on the back of the tunic just below the collar; signs worn in this position were generally regimental insignia. The flash on the helmet bears the letters 'WH'. This Yeomanry unit took part in the advance on Jerusalem as part of the 231st Infantry Brigade of the 74th (Yeomanry) Division. This brigade had been formed in January 1917 from eighteen dismounted Yeomanry regiments,

**Troops embussing at Arras on returning from the capture of Monchy-le-Preux by the 37th Division on 11 April 1917. (IWM)**

including twelve which had already served at Gallipoli. Given the unit's infantry role, the red grenade is probably a 'bomber's' distinction. After taking part in the attack on Beersheba and the capture of Jerusalem, the division embarked for France in May 1918.

*G1 Private, 'A' (1st) Battalion, Tank Corps; fighting order, France, 1917*

This new arm was formed from volunteers and utilised a number of innovations to the standard uniform. Until 1917 the Corps had no badge of its own and the men continued to wear their old regimental badges. A white worsted badge representing a Mk. I tank was issued and worn on the right upper sleeve of the tunic (*vide* a General Routine Order of 7 May 1917) and is still worn today by all ranks of the Royal Tank Regiment. In January 1917 coloured slip-on shoulder strap bands were introduced to identify the battalions of the Corps: 'A' = red, 'B' = yellow, 'C' = green, 'D' = blue, 'G' = red/green and 'H' = red/blue. In the tanks the

crews wore masks fashioned from chain mail to protect their faces from sparks and fragments—the enemy used armour-piercing machine gun ammunition, and on top of this, the engines were largely unguarded and were mounted in the centre of the fighting compartment. This private wears shorts—more common than might be supposed in the French summer—and 1914 leather equipment with a pistol and cartridge pouch. The ribbon of the Military Medal is worn on the left breast.

*G2 Driver, Royal Field Artillery, Divisional Artillery, 51st (Highland) Division; France, 1917*

This soldier is dressed in cavalry style and carries the haversack, waterbottle, and '08 pattern bandolier (five pouches at front only): artillerymen serving the guns or on battery duties were ordered to carry fifty rounds of rifle ammunition. The Royal

(Left) Group of Machine Gun Corps officers in typical dress with trench cap, service dress jacket, cord pantaloons, puttees and brown ankle boots, gaiters or high boots in various forms. As the war progressed front-line officers began to adopt other ranks' equipment, and on occasion, other ranks' jackets, to confuse enemy snipers. (Right) is a group of officers photographed behind the lines in 1917. The officer in the centre background seems to have a regimental badge on his steel helmet. They carry the box-type respirator. All have other ranks' '08 equipment, except the right hand seated figure, who wears 1914 leather equipment (R. Marrion)

Artillery's brass badge is worn on the cap, and the shoulder titles read 'RFA'. The famous sign of the Highland Division is worn high on each sleeve. There is a stout leather protector encasing the right leg, to prevent crushing when riding the gun-team horses.

*H1 Lewis gun 'No. 2', 2nd Battalion, Duke of Wellington's Regiment, 10th Brigade, 4th Division; France, 1918*

This soldier wears full marching order with the later, box-type respirator (SBR) slung over the head and resting on the large pack—a popular method of carrying it. He is armed with a revolver carried in an open holster, with '08 web or leather equipment. A blanket is strapped round the outside of his pack. During the war it became necessary to distinguish brigades and divisions quickly, and a system of signs was introduced which were displayed on the upper sleeves and/or on the steel helmet. This soldier wears a cut-out silhouette of his divisional sign, a stylized ram's head seen full face on, in green; it was worn in various different colours by other units of the division. He also wears red patches on helmet and sleeve, which are probably a

brigade distinction. On the lower left sleeve are a long service and good conduct chevron, and a gold wound stripe.

With the introduction of the Lewis gun a method had to be devised for the 'No. 2' in the LG section to carry the drum magazines easily. The Mills Factory designed a set of webbing comprising four magazine carriers each holding two drums. The circular carriers each had a pair of braces worn in conjunction with the standard webbing, the carriers being linked by means of straps on the back. The gun itself was carried on a special sling lined with asbestos, to protect the gunner from the heat of the weapon after prolonged firing.

*H2 Private, 1st Battalion, Essex Regiment, 37th Division; France, 1918*

This soldier is in fighting order, and the large pack is not worn. The haversack is carried on the back instead, with a waterproof groundsheet rolled and buckled to the belt support straps. Iron rations (1lb. of biscuit, 1 tin of 'bully', 2oz. sugar and $\frac{1}{4}$oz. tea)

Unique studio portrait of an original member of the Tank Corps. This youthful private wears the cap-badge of the Machine Gun Corps and 'HMGC' shoulder titles identifying him as a member of the Heavy Machine Gun Corps (Tanks). The photograph obviously marks his successful completion of training, as he has the tank emblem on his right sleeve, awarded by an order of 7 May 1917. As the Heavy Machine Gun Corps formed part of the Machine Gun Corps until July 1917, this dates the photograph quite closely. The tunic buttons are still the General Service pattern, bearing the Royal Coat of Arms. (Courtesy J. Woodroff)

were carried in the haversack together with any unconsumed part of the normal daily ration. Also carried were a knife, fork and spoon, a tin of oil, and flannel 'four by two' cleaning cloth for the rifle (the .303 SMLE Rifle No. 1 Mk. III, with an 18in bayonet).

This unit formerly served in the 29th Division, at which time a red triangle was worn on the front of the helmet and a red diamond on its sides. The triangle was repeated on the sleeves one inch from the shoulder seam, and the diamond on the back of the tunic below the collar. The coloured bands on the shoulder straps identify the company; 'W' Company wore blue, 'X' Company wore red, 'Y' Company wore mauve and 'Z' Company wore green. The yellow horseshoe is the divisional sign, the brown rectangle on the sleeve probably the brigade sign, and the helmet marking probably the regimental sign within the formation.

### H3 Stretcher Bearer, RAMC, 42nd (East Lancs) (TA) Division; France, 1918

In addition to the normal '08 equipment, bearers and medical orderlies carried a leather and webbing first-aid satchel. This bearer, in marching order wears a Red Cross brassard on the left arm. The sign of this division was a red-over-white halved diamond, and each unit wore a diamond in a different colour combination with a numerical identification superimposed on it. Units also wore diamonds in varying colours below the collar on the back of the tunic. Medical personnel sometimes wore circular red-cross-on-white badges on both upper arms. This man wears overseas service chevrons on his right lower sleeve.

This well-travelled division was one of the first of the Territorial Army to go abroad. It sailed to Egypt in 1914, and in February 1915 was fighting the Turks along the Suez Canal. In May 1915 it went to Gallipoli; it was in Sinai in 1916, and returned to France in March 1917.

Western Front, summer 1918; a private of the South Staffordshires wearing shirtsleeves, shorts, cap and puttees as he escorts prisoners to the rear during the battle of Albert. (IWM)

# Notes sur les planches en couleur

**A1** La tenue de service de kaki de 1902, portée avec une casquette de laine à la place de la casquette normale, et avec poches spéciales pour grenades à main, une massue, et un couteau pour usage pendant 'razzias' des tranchées. **A2** Prenez note d'insignes de grade d'officier sur manchette, écussons de régiment sur casquette et sur col, et un écusson divisionnaire sur les hautes manches. **A3** *Highland* régiments portaient un tablier de kaki sur le jupon et une couverture de kaki sur le *bonnet* bleu. La crinière rouge est une distinction de régiment.

**B1** Les insignes divisionnaires sont portés sur le brassard de cet officier d'état-major. Il porte le style de tunique écossais, avec coins arrondis aux pans au devant; culottes à l'écuyère de tartan; et la casquette Glengarry de régiment. **B2** Écussons de col en couleurs différentes identifiantes l'arme étaient la distinction des officiers d'état-major. **B3** Prenez note des écussons de col et d'insigne sur casquette de général.

**C1** Insigne de régiment sur casque et col; répétés sur les chevrons de la manche droite à la mode de cavalerie. Les chevrons sur la manchette droite indiquent service d'outre-mer, et les écussons du col de son régiment attachés en épingles au bord de son grand chapeau mou à larges bords. **C2** Une fraction au service en Grande-Bretagne en faction de défense côtière, ce bataillon porta un ruban de casquette vert, et grand équipement d'infanterie. **C3** Ce régiment de Yeomanry fut au service en France; les insignes de grade et les boutons argentés furent une distinction de régiment.

**D1** Le casque fut distribué en 1916. Le triangle rouge sur les manches identifie 168th Brigade. Insignes de col sont de régiment, et le cordon de la Territorial Decoration est porté sur le sein gauche. **D2** Insigne de régiment sur casque, en contrefaçon de la crinière jaune portée sur garniture de tête à grande-tenue. Insigne divisionnaire sur épaule; *webbing* fourniment complet de toile du 1908. **D3** Vêtements et bottes protecteurs typiques pour campagne en hiver dans les retranchements.

**E1** Version à poids leger de '*khaki drill*' de tenue d'officiers, avec insignes de grade sur les pattes d'épaule à la place sur les manchettes. La pièce noire sur le revers du casque et les cordons sur le dos de tunique furent distinctions de régiment; la pièce de manche noire et blanche est une distinction de brigade. **E2** Insigne de bataillon sur casque; même style de chemise bleue-grise comme celles portées par simples soldats mais différents de les leurs celle-ci tient un col. **E3** La 'P' se réfère à 'Pionniers'—plus tard elle fut portée sans le fond de losanges bleus. **E4** Le triangle noir sur la toile de cou piquée est un insigne de brigade.

**F1** Insigne de bataillon sur casque; *marching order* fourniment complet. **F2** Fourniment et tenue à la mode de cavalerie pour ce soldat de Détachement de Transport, mais avec les écussons du col de son régiment attachés avec épingles au bord de son grand chapeau mou à larges bords. **F3** Le 'château' rouge sur le chapeau est une distinction de régiment, le galon rouge sur les épaules un insigne divisionnaire. Un de plusieurs régiments de cavalerie démonté de voluntaire lequel fut au service comme infanterie dans la 74eme Division.

**G1** L'écusson de char d'assaut blanc sur la manche identifie le Corps de Char d'Assaut, le galon rouge sur la patte d'épaule le 1er ou 'A' Bataillon. Pantalons courts furent souvent portés en l'été en France, et le fourniment est le type de cuir de 1914. **G2** Ce soldat d'Artillerie à Cheval porte tenue et fourniment à la mode de cavalerie, et une jambière de cuir pour protéger la jambe contre écrasement par les chevaux.

**H1** Les pièces rouges sur casque et sur manche sont un insigne de brigade, et les insignes verts sur l'épaule est un insigne divisionnaire. Il porte les poches de toile pour les magasins ronds de la mitrailleuse Lewis. **H2** Galons colorés sur les pattes d'épaule identifient la compagnie dans le bataillon—'W' bleu, 'X' rouge, 'Y' mauve, 'Z' vert. Le fer de cheval jaune est l'insigne divisionnaire, la pièce brune un insigne de brigade, et les insignes de casque identifient le régiment. **H3** L'insigne divisionnaire fut un losange rouge-et-blanc, et chaque fraction dans la division porta un losange sur la manche en couleurs identifiantes l'arme, et avec un numéro identifiant la fraction.

# Farbtafeln

**A1** Der 1902 Dienstanzug aus Khaki mit einer Mütze aus Wolltuch anstatt der normalen Mütze mit Schirm getragen, und mit Spezialpatronentaschen für Hand-granaten, eine Keule, und ein Messer für Schützengrabenangriffe. **A2** Bemerken Dienstgradabzeichen Offiziers auf Stulpe, Regimentsabzeichen auf Mütze und Kragen, und Divisionsabzeichen auf Oberärmeln. **A3** *Highland* Regimente trugen eine Schürze aus Khaki über dem Schottenröckchen und einen Bezug aus Khaki über dem blauen *bonnet*. Der rote Federbusch ist eine Regimentsauszeichnung.

**B1** Die Divisionsabzeichen werden auf der Armbinde dieses Stabsoffiziers getragen. Er trägt die schottische Mode Waffenrocks mit abgestumpften Ecken auf den Vorderrockschössen; Reithose aus Schottentuch; und die Regiments-Glengarry-Mütze. **B2** Kragentuchstreifen in verschiedenen Farben nachweisend Waffengattung waren die Auszeichnungen Stabsoffiziere. **B3** Bemerken Kragentuchstreifen und Mützeabzeichen Generals.

**C1** Regimentsabzeichen auf Helm und Kragen; nochmal auf den Unteroffiziertressen auf dem rechten Ärmel in der Mode Kavallerie. Die Abzeichen auf der rechten Stulpe bezeichnen Auslandsdienst und auf dem linken Ärmel sind das Schütze-abzeichen und ein goldenes Verwundetenabzeichen. **C2** Ein Verband im Küsten-verteidigungsdienste in Britannien trug diese Abteilung eine grüne Mützebande und Infanteriausstattung. **C3** Dies Yeomanry Regiment diente in Frankreich; die silberfarbige Dienstgradabzeichen und Knöpfe waren Regimentsauszeichnungen.

**D1** Der Helm wurde in 1916 ausgegeben. Das rote Dreieck auf den Ärmeln weist 168th Brigade nach. Kragen- und Achselstück-abzeichen sind vom Regiment, und das Ordensband des *Territorial Decoration* wird auf der linken Brust getragen. **D2** Regimentsabzeichen auf Helm als Nachahmung von dem gelben Feder-busch auf Galakopfbedeckung getragen. Divisionsabzeichen auf Schulter; ausführliche 1908 *webbing* Ausstattung aus Drillich. **D3** Typische Schutz-Kleidung und -Stiefel für Winterkampf in den Schützengraben.

**E1** Leichtversion aus '*khaki drill*' Offiziersuniform, mit Dienstgradabzeichen auf den Achselstücken anstatt der Stulpen. Der schwarze Tuchstreifen auf der Rückseite des Helms und die Odensbände auf dem Rück des Waffenrocks waren Regimentsauszeichnungen; der schwarze und weisse Ärmeltuchstreifen ist eine Brigadeauszeichnung. **E2** Abteilungsabzeichen auf Helm; gleiche Mode blaugrauen Hemd wie diese von gemeinen Soldaten getragen aber verschieden von ihnen hat dieses einen Kragen. **E3** Der 'P' verweist an 'Pioniers'—später wurde es ohne dem Hintergrund blauer Rauten getragen. **E4** Das schwarze Dreieck auf der gesteppten Schutztuch am Rück des Hals ist ein Brigadeabzeichen.

**F1** Abteilungsabzeichen auf Helm; ausführliche *marching order* Ausstattung. **F2** Ausstattung und Uniform in der Mode Kavallerie für diesen Soldat der Truppen-abteilung, aber mit den Kragenabzeichen seines Regiments an der Krempe sines breitkrempigen Schlapphut festgehalten. **F3** Das rote 'Schloss' auf dem Hut ist eine Regimentsauszeichnung, der rote Streifen auf den Schultern ein Divisionsabzeichen. Ein vieler angesessenen Freiwilligenkavallerie-regimente das als Infanterie in der 74ten Division diente.

**G1** Das weisse 'Panzer'-abzeichen auf dem Ärmel weist das Panzerkorps nach, der rote Streifen auf dem Achselstück die 1ste oder 'A' Abteilung. Kurze Hose wurden oft in Sommer in Frankreich getragen, und die Ausstattung ist die 1916 Mode aus Leder. **G2** Dies Soldat reitender Artillerie trägt Uniform und Ausstattung in der Mode Kavallerie, und einen Beinschutz aus Leder, um das Bein vor Quetsche von den Pferden der Geschützbedienung zu schützen.

**H1** Die rote Tuchstreifen auf Helm und Ärmel sind ein Brigadeabzeichen, und die grüne Abzeichen auf der Achsel ist ein Divisionsabzeichen. Er trägt die Patronentaschen aus Drillich für die runde Magazine des Lewis-Maschinenegewehr. **H2** Farbige Streifen auf den Achselstücken weisen die Kompagnie in der Abteilung nach—'W' blau, 'X' rot, 'Y' mauve, 'Z' grün. Das gelbe Hufeisen ist das Divisionsabzeichen, der braune Tuchstreifen ein Brigadeabzeichen, und die Abzeichen auf Helm weisen das Regiment nach. **H3** Das Divisionsabzeichen war rote-und-weisse Raute und jeder Verband in der Division trug eine Raute auf dem Ärmel, in Farben, die Waffengattung weiste nach, und mit einer Nummer, die der Verband weiste nach.